Doing Effective Fieldwork

Doing Effective Fieldwork

A Textbook for Students of Qualitative Field Research in
Higher-Learning Institutions

Elia Shabani Mligo

RESOURCE *Publications* · Eugene, Oregon

DOING EFFECTIVE FIELDWORK
A Textbook for Students of Qualitative Field Research in Higher-Learning
Institutions

Resource Publications
An Imprint of Wipf and Stock Publishers
199 W. 8th Ave., Suite 3
Eugene, OR 97401

www.wipfandstock.com

ISBN 13:978-1-62032-793-7

Manufactured in the U.S.A.

To
Prof. Halvor Moxnes
University of Oslo Norway
My superior in research and teacher of disciplined
Academic life

Contents

Foreword

ELIA SHABANI MLIGO'S BOOK is long overdue. It observes what is gradually becoming a crisis, namely "doing effective research"; be it fieldwork, or analysis of secondary literature in libraries among scholars. Why universities and colleges are obligated to position research at the centre of their academic work? With particular reference to our times, the danger for not doing proper research is exacerbated by two factors: First, the proliferation of information through the internet websites such as *Wikipedia* and *Google* and many others which have made what seems to be distant information closer at home.

Without taking away the role and usefulness of the internet in research, however, the danger lies in the fact that scholars might see the internet as the only tool for doing research without bearing in mind that the information on the various websites needs to be verified through and supplemented by proper field research or by other research-oriented academic means. The second danger is that globalization seems to provide an assumption that research is no longer necessary due to the coming together of people. Research has seemly been associated with what people view as foreign and distant. In this case, globalization provides an assumption that research is no longer important since what was used to be distant and foreign is now our neighbor.

Through the step-by-step presentation of the way to do research in this book, Elia Shabani Mligo reminds us that the danger due failure to embark on proper research is catastrophic and the results take centuries to undo. On this issue examples are not far to see. Historically, the misrepresentation of non-western societies by missionaries, travelers, and arm-chair western anthropologists as being primitive, backward, and uncivilized, due to lack of proper research, resulted in negative descriptions which culminated in heinous acts in the history of humankind such as slavery and colonization. Today, there are more reasons to avoid such ancient historical pitfalls given the contemporary challenges such as homosexuality, migration, tribalism and other related issues. In this book, Mligo reminds the academic community that research must be thorough and without bias in bringing information to people because failure to do proper research is detrimental not only to the standard of education but also to the cohesion of humanity at large.

However, a sufficient treatment of the central topic is no easy matter. How can one do research? How can we be ethical and responsible in the manner we conduct research? These are some of the central questions in every serious research work. In this book, Mligo develops an extended and comprehensive discussions of this matter. The following four aspects stand out as the main pillars in conducting proper research. First, Mligo reminds us that in doing research we must aim at articulating the world, the experiences and the events from the point of view of the others, namely the respondents. Mligo cautions us that we do not carry out research in order to be polemic or to endorse previously held views. Instead, research is sympathetic to the views of the respondents; it must have phenomenological orientations.

Embarking on such a task is not easy because as researchers we possess our own idiosyncrasies and perceptions. The possession raises further challenges: How does an outsider look and describe a phenomenon from the perspective of an insider? Simply put, how does an outsider become an insider? Historically, this challenge was solved by learning the language of informants and staying in the fieldwork for an extended period. However, due to globalization, and that most people carry out fieldwork in their own communities, it is imperative to have good informants. The other side of this challenge is about the way an insider can objectively report and describe a phenomenon for the outsiders who are completely out of touch with events under discussion? The danger of being an insider researcher that researches in one's own village, town, city or country is that one becomes blind to certain issues by taking them for granted. In the same vein, an insider researcher tends to use terms and expressions that outsiders might not understand. The dictum is that an insider researcher must pay attention to details and provide sufficient descriptions of the events.

Related to the quest to represent the world from the perspective of the respondents is the problem of language. Most African researchers, for example, use English as second language thus facing the challenge of using the right adjectives to describe the phenomenon and to communicate to the global world. Given that language is embedded with the worldview and idioms of a people, the problem of not being non-English native-speakers results in the challenge of articulation. Mligo reminds us of the importance of subjects and discourses such as cultural studies, postcolonialism and poststructuralism in exposing the hegemony and imperial dominance of English and how English has robed most researchers, especially those from Africa, of the ability to carry out research using their own native languages.

Secondly, in this book Mligo reminds us that research must be holistic. Being holistic simply means that the subject or topic under discussion must not be studied in solitude. In other words, an event is part of a ripple of social events. An event is connected to several other events and issues affecting the community. For example, one cannot research on the social challenges caused by HIV and AIDS without connecting them to other social issues such as poverty, economic decline and lack of economic decline. Similarly, the challenge of migration cannot be studied while being blind of perennial social issues such as hunger and unemployment. A holistic research, as Mligo reminds us, looks at the way in which the topic under discussion is connected and is intertwined with numerous other issues affecting the community.

Third, through various examples, Mligo shows us that research is a painful undertaking. The pain is incurred not due to scarcity of information or resources to substantiate the claims of the research agenda, rather due to the rigorous and innovative journey leading the researcher into producing something new and significant. Many scholars avoid carrying out research because they fear pains associated with doing research. It is easy to be comfortable and to recycle what we already know. Proper research is a rigorous task that involves testing hypotheses and even critically questioning some established truths. Failure to confront the pain engendered by doing research scholars deprive their communities of new information and development.

Last, but not least, Mligo cautions us that the data and conclusions reached through field research belong to respondents. This is where research differs from journalism. In journalism, the focus is the consumers or the readers, but in research the researchers are accountable to people from whom they gathered the information. Placing the informants as custodians of the research is a guard against the problem of misrepresentation. Researchers must know and acknowledge that they are accountable to people from whom they gathered the information by respecting their views and their integrity.

By producing such mammoth work, Mligo challenges the academic community of the centrality of research in the production of knowledge and the development of society. I strongly guarantee this book to be one of the primary texts for researchers and scholars at both college and university levels.

Zorodzai Dube (PhD) August 2012
University of South Africa
Pretoria, South Africa

Preface

GRASPING LIVED CULTURES IN order to articulate people's experiences presents to us with images of both the spectacular and the ordinary. This necessitates the question of research and its processes. But everyday life presents to us with loosely defined meanings of research. Elia Shabani Mligo in this book embarks on a journey to demystify for both novices and experts alike what field research really is.

Doing effective Fieldwork clarifies various technical aspects and rules of research while narrowing itself down to the area of qualitative research and its corresponding techniques. In recent years, studies in qualitative research have indicated that implicit in its range of methods is its epistemology; that the world is to be discovered. More recently, however, qualitative research has been undertaken with the care it needs thus addressing questions of sources of knowledge and ways of knowing: "Where do we speak from?"

The book by Mligo you are about to read provides us a richer picture of field research. Certainly, in this book you shall see processes that enable one to locate instances in order to generate materials from the field. Mligo offers practical guidance on the craft of research from formulating the topic to presenting it in a written form. Further, he articulately delves into ethical concerns relating to acquisition of research data. He then convincingly sums up with the way research findings may be communicated clearly. His treatment of the process of writing a well organized research report is commendable as many books on research tend to present very limited amount of materials on the writing processes.

Mligo provides us with key questions in the research process. The chapter highlights and study questions in this book present to readers possibilities of clear moments for reflection. These highlights will especially be helpful to both tutors and lecturers teaching research methods in colleges and universities.

Students who want to do empirical research will also find here a sufficient guide to research methods and methodologies to enable them ask key questions for effective research. Needless to say, this book by Mligo is a very important step for the many students taking masters' level, PhD level and even beyond. Definitely, this book will help us along the road of being effective in our research practices!

Loreen Iminza Maseno (PhD) August, 2012
Chairperson,
Department of Religion, Theology, and Philosophy,
Maseno University,
Maseno Kenya

Introduction

RESEARCH IS PART AND parcel of human existence. Human beings always doubt about existing phenomena, especially those taken for granted in societies. A normal human mind is a curious mind, a mind which always longs for knowledge and solutions to existing problems. In this case, research endeavors to satisfy human curiosity and inquisitiveness by trying rigorously to respond to perennial questions: What, why, where, when, and who. This means that research is not a simple and easily understandable concept. It is a wide concept which embraces different practices, at different places, and within different time frames. However, in resent years there has been a growing interest in fieldwork among students and researchers. Yet, there have also been a limited number of literatures that try to address this subject properly, especially to beginners in research.

This book is a simplified one. It is convenient to both beginners and experienced researchers in their field research enterprises. It focuses mainly on one type of research, that is, qualitative field research as a naturalistic study. The main objectives of this book are twofold: First, to enable researchers (both novices and experienced ones) irrespective of their disciplines, comprehend qualitative field research and its subsequent techniques; and second, to familiarize them to the various processes involved in field research in the post-modern paradigm so that they can use these processes in their own field research projects. Therefore, through the chapter highlights and study questions provided at the end of each chapter, this book is mostly a self-study textbook to be used by all serious qualitative researchers that aim at accomplishing their research projects successfully.

The book is organized in a way that is simple and easy to follow. It has ten chapters that are well arranged and with a coherent logic. Each chapter ends with some highlights and study questions to help readers revise and contemplate on what they have studied in the chapter. The first chapter introduces the reader to two confusing concepts, "scholarship" and "research," as conceived in academic life. The chapter discusses the meanings of the two concepts and the way they relate to each other. The second chapter discusses three important aspects in research: Research questions, theory, and strategy. The chapter assesses the role of each aspect in conducting field research. The third chapter looks at some rules of research and their place in this current postmodern paradigm and context of research. Therefore, these three chapters are introductory chapters to situate the researcher and orient the reader into the preliminary concepts in the field research process.

Chapter four dwells mainly on the concept of fieldwork and its relation to qualitative research. The chapter deals with qualitative field research and its distinctive features. Through this chapter the reader begins to immerse oneself into the main focus of the book. Chapter five provides the reader with some techniques about selecting a significant research problem to be used in conducting effective qualitative field research. It explains some of the ways in which the researcher can use to survey sources for the sake of identifying an area which is not yet researched; and the way that the researcher can use to define the problem identified. Chapter six is concerned about the way to deal with secondary sources. The chapter examines the way in which the researcher can survey the existing knowledge. The main purpose of this chapter is to show the way in which the researcher can deal with what others have done about the topic and what they have not done. Therefore, the chapter discusses how the researcher can review the relevant existing literature in order to see what he/she will contribute to existing knowledge.

Chapter seven looks at ways to identify a suitable qualitative field research design and how designing research mainly bases on the various existing traditions and paradigms of field research. More specifically, the chapter introduces post-modernism as a current paradigm into which researchers work. Through the presentation of the various features of the post-modern era, the chapter argues that doing qualitative field research in this postmodern era means many things to many people according to place, time, and existing conditions.

Chapter eight deals with some ethical issues that the researcher has to take into account when doing qualitative field research. Human beings involved in the research process need respect and integrity. This chapter discusses the ethical issues which the researcher needs to bear in mind when conducting field research in order to protect participants from physical and psychological harm. Therefore, this chapter leads the researcher towards recognizing his/her role towards the integrity of other people in his/her field research.

Chapter nine is concerned about the acquisition of research data. The chapter tries to respond to the question: *How* can the researcher access information from the research area? It discusses the various instruments used in qualitative field research in order to obtain the needed information from participants. The chapter also discusses the advantages and disadvantages of those instruments in relation to the current research context. Therefore, this chapter introduces the reader to important methods or ways through which the required information can be accessed.

Chapter ten closes the book. This chapter is as important as is field research itself. It deals with communicating the findings of the research. It does not matter whether the researcher has acquired sufficient and convincing data to support his/her claim. The way this researcher presents, or organizes the evidence in order to answer his/her research question matters greatly. This chapter argues that a persuasive and convincing research report needs to be well-presented, well-argued and well-documented. Hence, this chapter deals with ways in which the researcher can present, argue his/her case, and document it according to the language and procedures recognized by other researchers.

As I stated earlier in this introduction, this book can serve as a self-study guide aiming at illuminating researchers to develop their field research projects in a meaningful and logical way. The book serves as a textbook to be used by individual or group studies for beginners in undergraduate and postgraduate researches in all academic disciplines. At the end of each chapter there are some highlights of main points of issues discussed in the chapter and some study questions which are helpful tools to remind the researcher about what has been learnt. Therefore, the book will prove to be essential for students who are privately and seriously engaged in field study.

However, experienced researchers will also find solace in this book in matters that are always neglected but are highly important. Teachers of research in universities and collages will also find this book useful as one of their tools for equipping their students with necessary issues in academic field research. Moreover, this book is aimed at anyone who is interested in academic field research work in all types of organizations and workplaces. For that matter, it is my sincere hope that all serious field researchers will find this book helpful in their research and writing tasks.

In addition, as Alley rightly says, "I wish I could tell you that this book will make your scientific writing easy. Unfortunately, that's not the way scientific writing is. Scientific writing is hard work. The best scientific writers struggle with every paragraph, every sentence, [and] every phrase. They must write, then rewrite, then rewrite again."[1] This means that scientific writing is the result of the writer's struggle with many drafts! It is the researcher's duty to hone it towards an appreciated work. The task of this book is to awaken the reader's inquisitive mind by providing clues of research to enable him/her to think and work in the process of researching and communicating the findings. Therefore, one expects the researcher to make the maximum use of materials put forth in this book in order to write and re-write his/her research report. After completing his/her report, the researcher needs to be proud of his/her own craft.

In fact, I am grateful to editors, typesetters, and proofreaders at Wipf and Stock, and all colleagues and friends at Kidugala Lutheran Seminary and at Iringa University College, Amani University Project at Njombe, who contributed in the various stages of this book. They encouraged me in times of despair, challenged me to make adequate presentation of the material, to revise the material critically, and to discard most of the redundant materials in order to make the work more precise. I respect their physical, mental, and psychological contributions towards this book. I heartily confess that their contribution is invaluable. May God grant each of them peace and still mind to continue with their searches for more understanding of the world in which we live.

---

1. Alley, *The Craft of Scientific Writing*, x.

Research and Scholarship in Academic Life

"Scholarship [is] interpreted as a process of making a contribution to society through the integration and dissemination of ideas and knowledge. (. . .) scholarship means bringing together everything you have done and disseminating it."

—BREW, *THE NATURE OF RESEARCH*, 35

"Research is the manner in which we solve knotty problems in our attempt to push back the frontiers of human ignorance."

—LEEDY, *PRACTICAL RESEARCH*, 4

Introduction

ONE OF THE SERIOUS questions in speaking about scholarship and research is, in most cases, connected with the place of each concept in a specialized academic community. What is 'scholarship' and what is 'research'? What is the relationship between the two concepts, that is, research and scholarship, in the life of the academic? In this chapter, I first show what is special in each concept and then survey the link between them.

The important thing is to discover the meaning of scholarship and its intertwinement with other aspects of academic life, for example research.

How can we define 'scholarship'? Is it an aspect generally known, or an aspect that can be defined according to a particular discipline or field of study? What about academic fields or disciplines where professionalism is more valued than scholarship? How can we draw the relationship between research and scholarship in those disciplines? In most cases, looking at the different emphases and the disappearance of distinguishing boundaries among disciplines, the questions of the relationship between research and scholarship are hard and disturbing.

Scholarship in Academic Life

The concept 'scholarship' is used to show a variety of activities that academics pursue in their lives. On the one hand, most academics have claimed their activities as being "for mere scholarship," that is, their works have not contributed something new in their disciplines and they still continue as such. On the other hand, the concept 'scholarship' has been used to indicate the amount of dignity and value that a particular academic holds in the academic community. In whatever the case, the above views indicate that 'scholarship' is an important aspect in academic life.

The Australian researcher Angela Brew, in her study of academic researchers and their view of scholarship noted: "at its most basic level, scholarship was perceived sorely as the background work as a foundation for research."[1] On the one hand, Brew found that scholarship implied dealing with the existing literature in order to understand and have a critical evaluation that lays a foundation for research.[2] Scholarship is viewed as being an important aspect in providing the context of research. Hence, scholarship is the existing academic context of a particular phenomenon and research is something new that fits in that context; it is what has already been done about a particular phenomenon in a particular discipline or field of study.

On the other hand, Brew found that scholarship does not end with understanding and evaluating the existing knowledge in order to provide a context for the new knowledge. Rather, it is also an addition of the new knowledge to the existing one. It is the contextualization of the new knowledge into the existing knowledge, the new knowledge that comes out as one tries creatively to understand the existing knowledge. It is both a

1. Brew, *The Nature of Research*, 34.
2. Ibid.

preparation for research and research itself.[3] In that case, scholarship is a 'voyage of discoveries' in academic life.

Furthermore, Brew's research noticed that scholarship has something more than 'preparation' for research and 'addition' of new knowledge to the existing knowledge. Scholarship has something to do with the 'dissemination' of the new knowledge. It has to do with publication and teaching of that knowledge. In this case, "Scholarship [is] interpreted as a process of making a contribution to society through the integration and dissemination of ideas and knowledge. (. . .) scholarship means bringing together everything you have done and disseminating it."[4] For Brew, dissemination can be achieved through the process of teaching, interacting with other people in conferences, seminars and through any other possible academic correspondence.[5]

The disturbing questions still remain: What is the place of research in academic life? How can we understand 'research' in the context of the above understanding of 'scholarship'? The above understanding indicates that research and scholarship are two distinct aspects in academic life; yet, they are inseparable in their praxis. In this case, scholarship involves scholarly research activities in the life of the academic. It concerns about "knowing how to: do competent research; read, interpret and analyse arguments; synthesize ideas clearly and systematically; and use your imagination."[6]

The British researcher Chris Hart contends that the most important element that demonstrates a 'good scholarship' is the ability of the researcher or scholar to 'integrate' ideas and theories from various fields of knowledge in order to bring about an illuminating understanding about a particular phenomenon. Hart states thus:

> A key element that makes for good scholarship is integration. Integration is about making connections between ideas, theories and experience. It is about applying a method or methodology from one area to another: about placing some episode into a larger theoretical framework, thereby providing a new way of looking at that phenomenon. This means drawing elements from different theories to form a new synthesis or to provide a new insight. It might also mean re-examining an existing body of knowledge in the light of a new development. The activity of scholarship is, therefore, about thinking systematically. It might mean forcing new typologies onto

3. Ibid., 34.
4. Ibid., 35.
5. Ibid.
6. Hart, *Doing Literature Review*, 8.

the structure of knowledge or onto a taken-for- granted perspective (. . .). Therefore, systematic questioning, inquiring and a scrutinizing attitude are features of a scholarly activity.[7]

For scholarship to be complete, therefore, it needs to include four important aspects as Boyer mentions them: The 'scholarship of discovery' where research is done for the sake of investigating for new knowledge, the 'scholarship of integration' whereby ideas are drawn from various disciplines and concepts in order to enhance knowledge, the 'scholarship of application' whereby the knowledge becomes beneficial to the surrounding society, and the 'scholarship of teaching' whereby scholars inspire new scholars and learn new trajectories from the interaction with students.[8]

The elements of a 'good scholarship' mentioned above are also the elements of a 'good research'. The above elements indicate that a good scholar is not the one that only deals with the existing knowledge but also that constantly longs to make discoveries of new knowledge through his/her endeavor to critically evaluate the existing knowledge and creatively discover new knowledge, which he/she contributes to the existing knowledge. The above unity between scholarship and research implies that scholarship without research and contribution of new knowledge to the existing knowledge is dead in itself and useless.

Research in Academic Life

Having discussed the efficacy of scholarship in academic life, we now turn our discussion towards what constitutes a research in particular. Machi and McEvoy illuminate us that "All successful research begins with inquiry. The researcher must have an inquiring mind, natural curiosity, and a fundamental need to learn and discover."[9] Machi and McEvoy continue: "The researcher must have an innate awareness of when present knowledge is insufficient and must have an intuitive sense of when something is missing."[10]

If the above statement by Machi and McEvoy provides us with an illumination about the nature of all research and the nature of the researcher, then we can ask, what is research all about? We can respond to this question

7. Ibid., 8–9.

8. Boyer, *Scholarship Reconsidered*, 16–25.

9. Machi & McEvoy, *The Literature Review*, 6.

10. Ibid.

by referring to the ideas of Paul D. Leedy. Leedy elucidates the meaning of research by noting what happens to students from the early stages of their academic life to the final university level that he considers as not being related to what research really is. Leedy notes:

> many students have labored under the delusion that looking up a few facts and writing them down in a documented paper constitutes research. Such activity is of course, no more than fact-finding and fact-transcribing. No amount of mere transfer of information from one place to another—even though the act of transportation is acknowledged by footnote—can be dignified by the term *research*. Transfer of information, transportation of fact from one place to another, is simply that, nothing more! Yet the strange misconception that fact transferral is research persists; and, what is even more disconcerting, is the aided and abated by the student teachers and professors as the student moves through the educational system from grade school to high school, high school to college, and even from college to graduate school. (. . .). The deception of the student is promoted at the college level by substituting merely a more glorified terminology. Fact transcription in college is frequently exalted by calling the end product as 'research paper,' a 'research report,' or 'research document,' without the student's having been given one iota of direction dealing with the specific requirements of basic research.[11]

Leedy's statement above prompts us towards stating clearly what research is and what is not.

What Research Is Not

As it has been indicated above, the word "research" has been so loosely defined in everyday life not only by students, but also by scholars in different fields of study. Leedy and Vyhmeister[12] suggest that we define the word 'research' by first looking at what is not research according to the general conducts of scientists and researchers:

11. Leedy, *Practical Research*, 4.
12. See Leedy, *Practical Research*; Vyhmeister, *Quality Research Papers*, 5–6.

a. "Research is not a mere collection of information from the field, library, or anywhere about a certain topic"

It is true that there is a collection of information during the research process. This collected information is the bases for analysis, interpretation, and discernment of the research findings. Nevertheless, one can hardly claim that this mere collection of information is 'research' in its wider sense. As Leedy has noted above, the collection of materials from the library can be a 'fact finding' or 'transfer of materials from one place to another', which is not actually 'research' in its real sense.

A student in a certain University College had this to say: 'I am very tired today. One of our professors in our Faculty ordered us to go to the library and do research about 'the role of human emotions in the learning process'. The professor ordered us to collect and present materials about that topic in class. Oh, we collected a lot of materials about human emotions'. Whose problem about research is this? Probably, it is the Professor's problem. The student's statement above indicates that the Professor hardly distinguished mere collecting of materials and presenting them in class and doing research.

Students can be ordered by their teachers to collect information from the library or any other place. That is worth of their duty. But that has been, in most cases, wrongly interpreted by those teachers who order students to go and collect materials. Most of them have considered such collection of materials as 'doing research'. Leedy warns us that though such collected materials are well-documented and well-reported, they can hardly be considered as 'research'; the activity done remains a mere transfer of materials from the place of collection to another place.

b. "Research is not mere transportation of facts from one location to another"

It is easy to claim that one has found something new in the library after having collected a number of facts and ideas from previous works or researches. This means that an individual can claim to have discovered something new after reading and collecting materials from the library. The main idea of this paragraph emphasizes that mere collection of materials from other researches can hardly be a full research in its general sense of the word. One competent student in a certain University completed the 'Research Paper' as his requirement for the completion of the semester. He collected various materials from the library, arranged them in a logical sequence, documented all the sources used, arranged all bibliographical entries in a proper alphabetical sequence. Hence, the student was convinced that she had exhausted all what was needed for a research work to write a research paper.

However, no place in that paper indicated the student's analysis, and interpretation of the collected materials. Neither was there any conclusion or recommendation from the obtained materials. This student was not far from genuine research; but his mere compilation of facts, his presentation of those facts with reference citations and arranging them in a series, no matter how appealingly neat the format, the student missed genuine research. A little farther, this student would have travelled from one world to another. He would have travelled from the world of mere transportation of facts from the library to the world of analysis and interpretation of those facts. The difference between the two worlds is what makes the distinction between mere transference of information and genuine research. This distinction is important to recognize in order to understand what research really means.

The most disturbing aspect in the statement of the student above is in the way most students and teachers think about research. Unfortunately, most students and teachers think that when they collect materials from libraries, arrange them in a proper manner, document their sources and list the required bibliography, they have accomplished what is required of research. Such activity is actually not research but 'fact transportation' or 'fact transcription' that needs further steps to 'research' proper.

In fact, research is not spending a considerable time hunting for related quotations from various sources and compiling them into a logical sequence. However, it is true that quotations are used to document the research argument, but such quotations are not research themselves. They are just evidences to make the research results concrete. A good research report uses quotations to support what the researcher presents from his research. Quotations help the researcher to demonstrate that what he/she concluded is based on reasonable evidences. Therefore, quotations are used for a special purpose in the research report, that is, to provide strength to the argument purported by the research report.

c. "Research is not just a defense of one's own convictions"

Every researcher has his/her own convictions which are held dear before approaching the research question. These convictions are the starting point towards the communication of the researcher's research truth. Though these convictions may be important to the researcher and his/her context, they may not necessarily be important to other researchers in their own contexts. This means that the researcher's convictions are not stable as truth because truth becomes unveiled through research. This means that truth is the sole concern of research. It longs to make it transparent, without hiding. Research endeavors to defend truth in whatever costs available. It does not defend the researcher's own convictions. In this case, the arguments which the researcher constructs in the research report need to be both sound and true.

d. "Research is not being polemical to other researchers' ideas"

The researcher needs to recognize his/her position in research and in the research report communicated to other people. He/she has also to acknowledge that the position that the researcher has cannot necessarily be the position of every person in the research community. The main objective of research is to communicate what the researcher thinks as being the truth for the wider knowledge; it does not intend fighting other people's ideas. In this case, the use of harsh language towards other people's ideas in research reports distorts the main concern of research.

What Research Is

It should still be remembered, however, that research has many meanings depending on who decides what research is. What we want to emphasize here is that there are so many things in everyday life that are considered to be research. We question the authenticity of what we see, we question the value of things when we do shopping, we check rates in various business goods and question their validity, we compare the prices of goods, we doubt the behavior around us in relation to what we are used to seeing. It is possible to imagine all these activities as being research because they are serious inquiries that long to enable someone to know something.

However, research has its beginning and its accepted rules to follow. Moreover, for Leedy, "Research is the manner in which we solve knotty problems in our attempt to push back the frontiers of human ignorance."[13]

---

13. Leedy, *Practical Research*, 4.

It is a process through which researchers attempt to achieve systematically, and with the support of data, the answer to a question, the resolution of a problem, or a greater understanding of a particular phenomenon.

This process, which mostly characterizes research, has eight distinct aspects according to Leedy. These aspects include the following:

i. *"Research originates with a question or problem in the researcher's point of view"*

To say that research originates with a question or problem is to look at both the world and human existence. We are surrounded by many unresolved questions around us. When people look at the world around them, they automatically see things that cause them wonder and raise questions: Why do people behave the way they do? Why are there many deaths due to malaria in this area? How can we improve the teaching leaning process in Secondary schools? What are the effects of deforestation in Sub-Saharan countries? These are some of the questions that can be raised when people look at the world around them. Such questions indicate the existence of problems that prompt us to undergo a particular process to find answers or solutions for them.

ii. *"Research requires identifying the problem, stating it unambiguously, and having a clear articulation of its goal"*

The mind of the researcher thinks about the problem in a wider sense. What the researcher needs to do after thinking about the problem is to identify and define the problem clearly. Defining the problem means setting it in specific margins. The researcher cannot deal with the whole idea he/she has in mind about the problem. He/she has to put it clear what exactly is the researcher going to work on. This is identifying and defining the problem.

By clear articulation of a goal, we mean the description of what the researcher intends to do with a particular identified problem. Any formal research must have a clear goal for doing it. The researcher cannot just collect information about the problem; the researcher needs to state the goal for researching about the problem according to his/her own point of view.

However, there is no one goal for all researchers concerning a particular problem. Every researcher approaches the problem with his/her own goal. The most important thing in making a good formal research is stating clearly the goal of the researcher in his/her approach to a stated problem.

iii. *"Research requires a specific plan of procedure in order to execute it"*

Formal research requires proper planning. It needs a clear statement of the way the researcher will execute the research. Planning of procedures means answering the question 'HOW'. Formal research should state how the research will go about investigating the problem or question at hand. In planning the procedures of research, questions such as: How can data be obtained, what are the samples to investigate, how will they be processed, and why use this or that instrument? These and other related questions are important in the planning of research procedures.

iv. *"Research usually divides the main problem into more manageable sub-problems"*

Problems to be investigated are in most cases wide and difficult to manage. Formal research divides larger problems into smaller manageable ones. Formal research does that in the conviction that the whole is made of its parts. Hence, investigating the parts will constitute investing the whole. Please look at the example below:

Larger Problem: Why are people stigmatized by their communities?
Smaller Problems: Why are women stigmatized due to their gender?

- Why are PLWHA stigmatized?
- Why are blind people Stigmatized?
- Why are people associating with PLWHA stigmatized?

In formal research, researchers need to take time to isolate the larger problem they need to investigate and its smaller problems. In doing that, research becomes plausible and manageable. If researchers do not take time to engage in this process, their research may be difficult to handle, and even unreliable.

v. *"Research is guided by appropriate hypotheses and is based upon obvious assumptions"*

After dividing the main problem into sub-problems that make the execution of research possible, formal research is, in most cases, guided by a hypothesis. What is a hypothesis? Leedy states: "A hypothesis is a logical assumption,[14] a reasonable guess, an educated conjecture which may give direction to your thinking with respect to the problem and thus aid in solving it."[15] Being a logical supposition, a reasonable guess, an educated conjecture regarding the problem under investigation, a hypothesis is not something new. It is an attempt by the researcher to account for the cause of the problem under investigation. The researcher constructs a problem through his/her investigation. He/she then divides the question into manageable problems, states the procedures to be followed in the investigation process, and constructs a possible cause of the problem (hypothesis).

In fact, it is not a guarantee that the hypothesis stated should be the true cause of the problem. What is close to the truth about the problem will be obtained after the collection, analysis and interpretation of collected materials. A hypothesis serves as a guide to the researcher in his/her research process. A hypothesis takes a stand that can be proved or disproved by the research data. The main function of the researcher after putting forth his/her hypothesis is to state, using the research data as evidence, whether the hypothesis is true or false, and to convince his/her readers in that position. Several hypotheses may be constructed concerning one problem, but they are just reasonable guesses to direct the researcher. However, some hypotheses may be true at the end of the research process, or none may be true. This is because the information collected may fail to support the stated hypothesis. In whatever the case, the hypothesis will have served its function, that is, directing and guiding the researcher in his/her research process.

14. Leedy also defines an 'assumption' as being "a condition which is taken for granted and without which the research effort would be impossible." (See Leedy, *Practical Research*, 6).

15. Leedy, *Practical Research*, 5.

> vi. *"Research accepts certain critical assumptions*
> *that are necessary for the research process"*

There are some assumptions which are like axioms in any research process. It is hard to approach a particular problem without some assumptions. An assumption is different from a hypothesis. While a hypothesis is a guess about a particular cause of the problem, an assumption is a certain condition which is taken for granted, without which research cannot proceed. The research rests on an assumption made. In that case, an assumption needs to be intelligible and acceptable by other researchers. It important that the assumption made is made open to others. This is important because the quality of the research will also depend on the prior assumptions the researcher had about the problem and the research process.

An example of an assumption can be obtained in laboratory works where various aspects are normally assumed constant. Moreover, in my doctoral study about People Living with HIV/AIDS (PLWHA) and the way they can overcome stigma, I made an assumption that "PLWHA are not empowered through non-HIV positive people taking the status of PLWHA upon themselves, nor through works of charity and caring concerns, but through PLWHA's own work with Jesus' narratives, and their integration of such narratives into their own situations of stigmatization."[16] This assumption served as the bases of my investigation of the way PLWHA can use biblical narratives to overcome the stigmatization surrounding them.

> vii. *"Research requires the collection and interpretation of data in*
> *attempting to resolve the problem that initiated the research"*

After the researcher has isolated the problem, divided it into appropriate sub-problems, posited reasonable questions or hypotheses, and recognized the assumptions that are basic to the entire effort, the next step he/she has to go is to collect whatever data that seem appropriate and to organize them in meaningful ways so that they can be analyzed and interpreted. It is in this way we consider research to be dealing with facts and their meaning.

Data or facts may be in the form of recorded events, happenings, observations or interviews. They may be in the form of content analysis from previous researches or hermeneutical works. But all these are only data, and are meaningful in themselves. They need interpretation. It should be

16. Mligo, *Jesus and the Stigmatized*, 11.

known that there is no one way, which is considered correct, to interpret the obtained data. The researcher and his/her mind are important tools to determine which way is appropriate and which way is not depending on the context of the researcher who embarked on the data collection process. In this case, the interpretation of data leading to certain conclusions is important in any research; and it is the work of the researcher depending on the whole process of research.

viii. "Research is, by its nature, cyclical; or more exactly, helical"

Speaking of research as being cyclical or helical is looking at the process of research itself. Research follows certain processes that are repeated in the cyclical form.

A. Research begins with a questioning mind that asks 'why' things appear the way they do and what causes them to appear like that. The idea begins in the mind of the researcher which leads him/her into further examination of the situation.

B. The researcher, basing on the questions about the existing situation, formulates a problem that needs a solution. This is what is called a 'statement of the problem'. Here the researcher *identifies* and *defines* the problem to be dealt with.

C. The researcher gathers data with respect to the problem under investigation through primary observation.

D. The data collection which the researcher makes through primary observation leads to a tentative solution. This tentative solution is a guess or hypothesis that guides the research process proper.

E. The need for more data emerges. The researcher extensively collects more data about the problem by using a selected research instrument.

F. The researcher analyses and interprets the collected data according to the context of the whole process of research.

G. After interpreting the data, the researcher hears what the data tells him/her in relation to the problem which the researcher initially embarked on. This may be a new discovery or a certain conclusion.

H. Up to this point, the researcher knows whether his/her hypothesis or guess of the solution he/she proposed is supported or not supported by the collected data.

I. Whether the data supports the hypothesis or not, the process of research has to start again by the researcher himself/herself, or by other researchers longing to indulge into some complex issues rose by the previous research. The process of research begins again because there is no true research which is conclusive and exhaustive. Research always begets research because any beginning research builds on the previous research or researches. This means that in the process of resolving the problem, the researcher may find other additional problems that need to be resolved, hence leading the researcher or other researchers to embarking into research.

The nine points listed above indicate that research cannot be tamed. Research can be done anywhere, any time, and by anybody. Research is a continuous process. This is because the questions raised about life are many and unanswered. What human beings do is to try answering such questions through research; and yet raising more questions for further research. In this case, we should better note that every researcher needs to make his/her research open to further investigation of the same issue. This means that, the same phenomenon can have different research results for different purposes.

Some More Ideas About Research

Despite the above ideas, there are still some more other ideas about research. According to Locke, Silverman and Spirduso: "Research begins when the investigator formulates a carefully defined question and then designs a systematic way to collect information that might provide an answer."[17] For these scholars, research is a planned and systematic process of answering questions according to rules that are particular to both a field of inquiry and a kind of research."[18] These scholars add: "research is a specialized enterprise that requires the skills and knowledge of a trained investigator. Research is a form of intellectual work, and it is done by people, not computers."[19]

17. Locke, Silverman & Spirduso, *Reading and Understanding*, 29–30.
18. Ibid., 31.
19. Ibid.

However, the above views on the meaning of research have recently been heavily debated. One such debate includes that of Angela Brew in her book *The nature of Research*. Brew contends that there has yet no developed definition to capture what really research is. She writes: "There is no one thing, no even a set of things which research *is*. It is obviously a complex phenomenon. It cannot be reduced to any kind of essential quality . . . any attempt to discuss research in general is at worst impossible and at best foolhardy."[20] What I see Brew depict to us in her assertion above is about the impossibility of having "the" research. The term 'research' is as fragile as its process of performing it. This means that research is research to particular contexts and to a particular understanding of people. Even among contexts, however, there are no clear boundaries that localize research within them alone. This is because there has been a sharing of ideas across boundaries, and hence, the inability to explain research in a more general sense is what makes it more complex to discuss about it.

In his more resent book *Essentials of Business Research* Wilson also purports that the definition of research is contested. However, Wilson provides an alternative to try defining it. He sees research to be comprising of three important aspects: First, research is 'a process of inquiry and investigation' because it has predetermined set of questions that the researcher seeks to obtain answers for them through a process of gathering data that help explain what the questions ask for. Second, research is 'systematic and methodical' because it is well organized and goes in a series of stages in order to be accomplished. Third, research aims at 'increasing knowledge' to the researcher, to the participants in the research, and to the academic community.[21] Therefore, according to Wilson, "Research is 'a step-by-step process that involves the collecting, recording, analyzing and interpreting of information."[22]

Conclusion

In this first chapter we concentrated sorely in examining the two aspects, that is, research and scholarship. The questions that were at the heart of this chapter are these: what is 'scholarship and what 'research is?' What is the relationship between the two aspects, and what is the place of each of

---

20. Brew, *The Nature of Research*, 21–22.

21. See Wilson, *Essentials of Business Research*, 2–3.

22. Ibid., 3.

them in the life of the academic? This chapter has therefore endeavored at responding to these questions.

It has been apparent from the discussion in this chapter that research and scholarship are interrelated aspects; yet they are different. Research has to do with the increase in new knowledge while scholarship has to do mainly with the dissemination of existing knowledge. In other words, scholarship is mainly the background for research. In this case, the understanding of research and scholarship as described in this chapter will help the researcher to indulge in more complex ideas relating to research enterprise.

Chapter Highlights

1. The term 'scholarship' means many things to many people: a variety of activities that are pursued by academics in their lives, the background work as a foundation for research, dealing with the existing literature in order to understand existing knowledge, the contextualization of new knowledge into the existing knowledge, dissemination of new knowledge, etc.

2. A good scholar is not the one that only deals with the existing knowledge, but also the one that longs to make discoveries of new knowledge through his/her efforts to critically evaluate existing knowledge and creatively discover new knowledge, which the scholar contributes to existing knowledge. This means that research and scholarship are inseparable.

3. All research begins with an inquiring mind to the researcher. It begins with critical questions about taken for granted phenomena, issues, or situations.

4. The real meaning of research is contested. However, it is possible to trace its meaning through analyzing what is really not research. In a more general definition, research is 'a step-by-step process that involves the collecting, recording, analyzing, interpreting information obtained, and disseminating the information in the form of a written research report.

Study Questions

1. By the use of as many other literatures as possible, and your own discipline of study, discuss the meaning of the terms 'scholarship' and 'research' in the life of the academician.

2. Research and scholarship are inseparable entities. Discuss this statement by the use of examples from your own field of study.

3. From the reading you have done in this chapter outline and discuss what is, and is not research.

4. What does it mean to say that research is cyclical in nature?

2

Research Question, Theory, and Strategy in Search

A research question for field research "is a question about the social world that you seek to answer through the collection of firsthand, verifiable, empirical data."

—CHAMBLISS & SCHUTT, *MAKING SENSE*, 22

"theories are versions of the world. These versions undergo a continuous revision, evaluation, construction and reconstruction. (. . .) theories are not (right or wrong) representations of given facts, but versions or perspectives through which the world is seen. (. . .). Theories as versions of the world thus become preliminary and relative."

—FLICK, *AN INTRODUCTION*, 43

The connection between theory and data from the field can be done through two ways. These ways are: "starting with a social theory and then testing some of its implications with data." Or "collecting the data and then developing a theory that explains it."

—CHAMBLISS & SCHUTT, *MAKING SENSE*, 25

Introduction

IN THE PREVIOUS CHAPTER, we discussed about the place of scholarship and research in academic life. We also defined research and the way we can distinguish it from none research actions. In this chapter, we discuss about the role of research questions, theories and research strategies in the execution of academic field research. We first define research question as described by research language, explain the characteristics of a good research question, the importance of research question and the way the research question is used in qualitative field researches. We also examine the use of theory in research. We discuss the meaning of a scientific theory, the importance of theory in research and the criteria for determining a useful theory. We conclude the chapter with a section on the discussion of the strategies of research. In this section we examine the important issues involved in deductive and inductive research strategies. We suggest in this section that most qualitative field researches use inductive strategies more than deductive. Therefore the main concern of the chapter is to show the importance of the three important aspects of research mentioned above: research question, theory, and strategy.

Research Question

What is a Research Question?

A research question, a socially oriented one, has to do with the empirical situation of people at a particular location. It "is a question about the social world that you seek to answer through the collection of firsthand, verifiable, empirical data."[1] The social research question with the above characteristics (firsthand, verifiable, and empirical) can emerge from various sources: from the researcher's experiences, from a certain social theory already propounded by social researchers, or from agencies that seek research to be done for a particular problem. Since society has diverse varieties of people and activities, a social question will be specific to a particular people, situation, or problem. People in a particular society do not have similar problems. Problems are different depending on their experiences of life.

Moreover, the emergence of the research question, the one that seeks to be answered, and that is meaningful and logically constructed is the result of an effort. It is the researcher's effort to construct such a question.

1. Chambliss & Schutt, *Making Sense*, 22.

Doing Effective Field Work

The researcher has to refine and reconstruct the possible research questions available in order to get one that is clear, researchable, meaningful and logical depending on a particular area of study. In this case, it is the task of the researcher to have a list of candidate questions which are narrowed down to get one that is more feasible and interesting for research purposes.[2]

What Characteristics Constitute a Good Research Question?

This is the first question every researcher can ask oneself before embarking into a research venture. Chambliss and Schutt quoting King, Keohane & Verba and Fraenkel, Wallen, and Hyun[3] have put forth four major characteristics: first, *feasibility* given the time and resources available; second, *social importance or significance*; third, *scientific relevance*, fourth, should be *ethical to participants* of the research, and fifth, *clarity*.

When speaking about feasibility we normally speak of the possibility to begin research at a particular problem in a particular social location with particular minimum available resources possible and finish it in a particular allotted time without possibilities for delay or failure. The research should be easily conducted without using much expense of time, money and energy of the researcher. Therefore, important questions about feasibility are the following: do I have the necessary sources to accomplish this research work? What about my qualifications, do I have sufficient qualifications to work with the problem at hand? What about time, do I have enough time to successfully work with the problem before the due date? What about financial expenses, do I have enough finances to pay for the costs pertaining my research process?[4]

When we speak of social importance (or significance) of the question we refer to the contribution that the question makes to the society if the answers for it are sought. "Will an answer to your research question make a difference in the social world, even if it only helps people understand a problem they consider important?"[5] This means that the question should be worth investigating because it has the potential of contributing important knowledge about the phenomenon it seeks to investigate. The worthiness of the question will depend mainly upon the context of the problem

2. Ibid.
3. Ibid., 22–23, and Fraenkel, Wallen & Hyun, *How to Design*, 28.
4. Cf. Vyhmeister, *Quality Research Papers*, 32.
5. Chambliss & Schutt, *Making Sense*, 23.

under investigation. The question needs to be significant to the researcher himself/herself, to the community investigated and to the academic community which the researcher belongs. The researcher should ask oneself about the question: how might the answers which will come out of this research question advance knowledge about the phenomenon? How might the answers to this research question improve human condition in my area of study or to people researched?

When we speak of the scientific relevance of the question, we speak of its ability to resolve an existing contradiction in a particular scientific theory or theories. "Does your research question help to resolve some contradictory research findings or puzzling issue in social theory? If so, your research question is scientifically relevant."[6]

When we speak of the research question being ethical to participants we mean that the investigation process about the question should not cause any physical or psychological harm to participants in the research. It should also not cause harm to the environment which these participants belong.

When we speak of the clarity of the research question we refer to the possibility of people to understand it. This means that the research question should be clearly understandable to most people who come across it. The question should state exactly what is being investigated. In this case, in order to get a question that is scientifically relevant, feasible, socially important, ethical and clear, the researcher will not avoid reading various literatures and conceptualizing about particular empirical situations. The review of literature will help the researcher to have a direction in his/her research question and to build his/her question in the experiences of previous researches.

What Is the Importance of a Research Question?

Research questions are crucial in research. They are crucial in the way to begin, proceed, and end one's research work. It hardly matters whether the researcher has a good research topic, has a good scholarship reputation, has well designed his/her research instrument (questionnaires, interviews and observations), has a well-funded project, a dissertation, and thesis or research paper supervised by a well trained researcher. If the researcher has not designed his/her research question well, he/she will be in a position to have his/her research unfocused; and hence, the researcher himself/herself

---

6. Ibid.

will understand very little as for what he/she collects research information.[7] This less knowledge will eventually lead the researcher into inadequate data analysis and reporting of subsequent findings.

Bryman outlines six important points that highlight the importance of research question in a process of research. According to him, research question is important "because it will:

- guide your literature search
- guide about your decision about the kind of research design to employ
- guide your decision about what data to collect and from whom
- guide your analysis of your data
- guide your writing up of your data
- stop you from going off in unnecessary directions and tangents."[8]

Bryman's highlights above indicate that mere collection of information without a focus through a specific research question leads to weak research report. This is because the researcher collects information without a clear vision as to what problem such information has to deal with. Therefore, the research question is the main focus of the research project. It is the one that holds the whole project together. Wilson rightly calls a research question 'the glue that holds the project together'.[9] Therefore, it is important that the research question is well-formulated and focused to what the research is interested to know in the topic which the researcher has designed by orienting it in or from the realm of previous researches.

Research Questions in Qualitative Fieldwork

Research questions in qualitative fieldwork are technical. They are oriented towards knowing *what* happens *there*, *how* individuals make sense of their lived experiences, and *why* things are the way they are. What we can say is that most research questions in qualitative fieldwork are of two types: explorative and descriptive questions. In order to allow research participants to describe about the social phenomenon under research, the researcher formulates the '*what*' question. This question longs to hear about what

7. Bryman, *Social Science Research*, 31.

8. Ibid.

9. Wilson, *Essentials of Business Research*, 3.

exists, its meaning to those who hold it and to other people that also adhere to it.

Example: What is the attitude of the Bena community towards unmarried young men and women?

In order to gain more understanding on the way the phenomenon is, the researcher asks the *'how'* question. The question explores the process of existence undertaken by the phenomenon. The 'how' question allows the research participants to describe the process or the way things go on in his/her context.

Example: How do teachers relate to students with skin abnormality in secondary schools within Njombe Region?

In order to know the rationale for the existence of what exists, the researcher formulates the *'why'* question. This question longs to explore phenomena that are always taken for granted. It explores the reasons for their existence, and for whose benefits.[10]

Example: Why do most people in villages prefer to drink unsterilized water from wells and streams?

Therefore, the three types of research questions are, in most cases, the ones that distinguish qualitative fieldwork from other types of researches.

Theories in Research

All research is based on various assumptions about the way the world is perceived and the way we should come to understand it. Nobody knows for sure the way the world is and the way we can best understand it. This has been the sole question and debate among philosophers and researchers for centuries now. Therefore, what research does is to examine the current approaches to the understanding of the world, and seeks to contribute to this understanding.

When the researcher formulates a good research question and orients his/her question in the previous researches, he/she works with theories already put forth about that particular problem or question. Theories are important because no research emerges from the air. Theories help to make

---

10. Hese-Biber & Leavy, *The Practice*, 40.

connections between the general understanding of social situation and researches that are currently being carried out and the particular social situations that exists in the time of research. This is possible because theories mostly emerge from scientific researches.

What Is a Scientific Theory?

Psychologists Kantowitz, Roediger III, and Elmes have the following definition: "A theory can be crudely defined as a set of related statements that explain a variety of occurrences."[11] According to educational researchers Gall, Borg, and Gall, "A theory is an explanation of observed events in terms of the structures and processes that are presumed to underlie them."[12] Ary, Jacobs, and Razavieh also point out that "A theory may be defined as 'a set of interrelated constructs (concepts), definitions, and propositions that present a systematic view of phenomena by specifying relations among variables, with the purpose of explaining and predicting the phenomena."[13] Bryman states that a theory "is an explanation of observed regularities (. . .)."[14] According to Chambliss and Schutt, "A social theory is a logically interrelated set of propositions about empirical reality (i.e., the social world as it actually exists)."[15]

However, according to Uwe Flick "theories are versions of the world. These versions undergo a continuous revision, evaluation, construction and reconstruction. (. . .) theories are not (right or wrong) representations of given facts, but versions or perspectives through which the world is seen. (. . .). Theories as versions of the world thus become preliminary and relative."[16] In understanding theory as a version of the world, Flick illuminates us that a theory is just an explanation of what is known about the world. It is just a starting point towards the search for what is not yet known.

Therefore, the above list of definitions and explanations imply that theories are not put forth in order to express an unchanging social world, or a necessarily correct situation; but, they are put forth in order to be tested whether they correspond to the reality as it exists in a particular time and

11. Kantowitz, Roediger III & Elmes, *Experimental Psychology*, 17.

12. Gall, Borg & Gall, *Educational Research*, 50 (emphasis is in original).

13. Ary, Jacobs, and Razavieh, *Introduction to Research*, 15.

14. Bryman, *Social Science Research*, 5.

15. Chambliss and Schutt, *Making Sense*, 23.

16. Flick, *An Introduction* 43.

place. Theories point to areas that researchers should direct their attentions and propositions that they should consider testing. This is because there are some situations that such promulgated theories cannot explain, especially in this current changing world.

An example of a social theory is the labeling theory. The labeling theory has to do with the question of deviance from what is deemed by the society as being the 'normal.' This means that there are actions that are considered normal and there are actions that are considered to be abnormal and hence are sanctioned by that society. What happens, according to this theory, is that when an individual is labeled, that person is considered to be a deviant from the normal, and the acts that that individual undergoes correspond to the deviant label attached to him/her. According to this theory, the labeled person and treated according to his/her label can respond in several ways: withdrawing from the group which labels, compensation, etc.

A theory is made up of small units and structures that are called *constructs*. The interrelation of such constructs in a particular theory is what makes a theory to be a theory. What is a construct? According to Gall, Borg and Gall, "A construct is a type of concept used by theoreticians to describe a structure or process that is hypothesized to underlie particular observable phenomena."[17] Elements such as stigma, experience, stereotype, label, etc., are some of the constructs in the labeling theory. The relationship among the mentioned constructs in a particular lived-reality is what constitutes a theory, an explanation about a particular lived-reality.

In What Way Is a Theory Important in Research?

Since any scientific understanding is tentative, theories are very important in research. Ary, Jacobs and Razavieh have described the importance of the formation of theories in their book *Introduction to research in education*. According to them, the work of researchers is too vast and scattered in a particular field of study. These collected facts and scattered facts need to be accumulated together, integrated and classified in order to have a meaningful explanation of what really exists. Therefore, "Theories are formulated to summarize and put in order the existing knowledge in a particular area."[18]

Another important function of theory is to provide a framework for researchers to orient their data. Researchers have to know how to organize

17. Gall, Borg & Gall, *Educational Research*, 50 (emphasis is in original).

18. Ary, Jacobs & Razavieh, *Introduction to Research*, 15.

their data according to the existing reality. Since theories explain existing realities, the organization of research data according to a particular theory enables the researcher to prove the correctness or incorrectness of that theory in its explanation of the existing reality. In fact, it "is in this way that we relate theory to the reality which it seeks to depict that we can hope to create this possibility of falsification and correction of assumptions about that reality."[19] Hence, by doing that the researcher gets a framework to organize the research results in a way that they provide an evidence for the truthfulness or falseness of the theory, or a ground for the modification or production of an alternative theory from the existing one.[20]

Some Criteria for a Useful Theory

In order for a theory to be useful it needs to meet at least the following criteria according to Ary, Jacobs, and Razavieh:[21] First, "A theory should be able to explain the observed facts relating to a particular problem; it should be able to propose the 'why' concerning the phenomena under consideration." In order for the theory to be understood it needs to be explained in simple language; and it should use the language related to what is going on in the area where it draws its concepts.

Second, "A theory should be consistent with observed facts and with the already established body of knowledge." The main concern of any theory is to account for what exists. However, no any theory can account on what exists without being consistent with what has already been theorized about the phenomenon. Therefore, consistence accounts for a theory that usefully explains about the newly discovered phenomenon.

Third, "A theory should provide means for its verification." This means that any theory should consider itself as a tentative explanation of the phenomenon that is subject to being tested for either rejection or modification. "A theory is useful or not useful, depending on how efficiently it leads to predictions concerning observable consequences, which are then confirmed when the empirical data are collected."

Fourth, "A theory should stimulate new discoveries and indicate further areas in need of investigation."

19. Barth, *Process and Form*, 8.

20. Kantowitz, Roediger III & Elmes, *Experimental Psychology*, 17–18.

21. Ary, Jacobs & Razavieh, *Introduction to Research*, 16.

Therefore, even though the above four points are not exhaustive to explain what makes a theory useful, they at least indicate that the usefulness of a theory is not determined by good description it provides or the type of phenomena being described, but by its efficacy to stimulate discoveries, its easy verification, the language it used and its consistence with what exists.

Strategies of Field Research

The labeling theory explained above, as any theory, is open to being tested and verified according to context and time. When this is done, the researcher connects the theory put forth with the empirical data obtained from fieldwork. The data that the researcher obtains from fieldwork provide the evidence of what is happening in the real world. Chambliss and Schutt assert the connection between theory and data from the field that can be done through two ways. These ways are: "starting with a social theory and then testing some of its implications with data." Or "collecting the data and then developing a theory that explains it."[22]

The first one is called *deductive research*, and according to Chambliss and Schutt, this is most often used in quantitative research methods. What is done in deductive research is that "The researcher, on the basis of what is known about in a particular domain and of theoretical considerations in relation to that domain, deduces a hypothesis (or hypotheses) that then must be subjected to empirical scrutiny. Embedded within the hypothesis will be concepts that will need to be translated into researchable entities."[23] Therefore, according to Bryman, the deductive research is arranged in the following way: Theory starts, then comes Hypothesis, comes Data collection, comes Findings, comes Confirmation or Rejection of the Hypothesis, then eventually, The revision of the existing theory.[24]

The second one is called *inductive research* and in most cases used in qualitative research methods. In the inductive research, theory becomes the outcome that emerges from the research conducted. It is the result of the way data collected explain about the existing situation in a particular community. In the words of Byman, the research "process of induction involves drawing generalizable inferences out of observations."[25] Therefore,

22. Chambliss & Schutt, *Making Sense*, 25.
23. Bryman, *Social Science Research*, 8.
24. Bryman, 9.
25. Ibid.

in the inductive research, research starts, then comes the findings, then comes formulation of the new theory.[26]

The deductive and inductive procedures or processes used in research are called *strategies, perspectives, or approaches of research*. In this case, whether one does an inductive or deductive research, or combining both of them needs to know well these strategies and the way they work in scientific researches.

Deductive Strategy

When considering about deduction in research, we primarily consider the already existing theory.[27] We consider the validity and verifiability of that theory. In order to find the validity and verifiability of the theory, the researcher will endeavor to look for the data that will confirm the validity of that theory. In this case, the most important thing that the researcher does is to take theory as his/her premise that will help in deducing the specific expectations depending on their context and time. These expectations are called *hypotheses*.

What is a hypothesis? In deductive research strategy a hypothesis is a statement, normally tentative, that tries to explain about a certain existing empirical situation. Gall, Borg and Gall have this definition: "A hypothesis is a testable prediction about observable phenomena that is based on a theory's constructs and their presumed relationships."[28] The above definition suggests that the hypothesis is always deduced from a theory. Since a theory is a more general statement, it cannot be easily tested; what is easily tested is a hypothesis or hypotheses that are deduced from the relationship of that theory's constructs. The hypothesis comprises of two parts called *variables*. Variables are constructs that have the possibility to vary in quantity or quality. Variables are important because they are the ones that the researcher measures their variation in quantity or quality. They are the ones that, due to their ability to vary in their quantity or quality, try to influence each other. If one variable grows large, the other weakens; or they may both increase at the same level. What the research takes into attention is the way one variable between the two influences the other.

---

26. Ibid., 10.

27. Cf. Ndunguru, *Lectures on Research*, 24.

28. Gall, Borg & Gall, *Educational Research*, 50.

Look at the example of Hypothesis below:

The *good performance of students* increases through *teachers' hard working.*

This hypothesis is measurable. In order to measure the truth of this hypothesis, teachers can reduce their working. Instead of working hard, they may reduce their working zeal. This will prove whether the increase of good performance of students depends on the hardworking of teachers. The variables for the above hypothesis are: *the good performance of students* and *the teachers' hard working.*

If the increase of the first variable depends on the increase of the second variable, the first variable is called a *dependent variable.* This is because its level of increase or decrease depends sorely on the level of the other variable. The dependent variable always predicts the results. The second variable explains the cause of that result. This is an *independent variable* because it does not depend on any other variable, but it is the causer of the level of the first variable.

In the above hypothesis, the good performance of students is a dependant variable because in order for it to change, it depends on the change of the second variable. *The teachers' hard working* is the second variable which causes the first variable to vary. Therefore the measurable nature of variables is the main feature that distinguishes them from other features like concepts or ideas which are immeasurable.

Inductive Strategy

Inductive is different from deductive research strategy. The word inductive comes from the verb '*induce*' which means to develop something from something. Inductive research strategy starts with the data that the researcher uses to develop a theory. It should be remembered that in deductive research, the researcher begins with a theory and finds data to test the validity of that theory. But in inductive research data are used to develop a theory. In this case, the experience of the researcher, his/her observation of reality, and his/her reflection upon it are the main bases for providing explanations to what exists.[29]

It is easier to formulate a research question in deductive research than in inductive researches. This is because the researcher questions the available theory; but in inductive research, the question emanates from the collection

29. Cf. Ndunguru, *Lectures on Research,* 222–33.

of data. In this case, the research question in inductive research strategies originates from the situation where the researcher collects data. What we can say about inductive strategy is that it pays more attention to specific contexts of phenomena and then looks at the general view of the phenomena.

Conclusion

In the whole of this chapter we concerned ourselves into the examination of three terminologies of research: research question, theory, and strategy. These aspects can be considered key aspects in the research process because they are the pillars of the research enterprise. Research question guides and determines the way data are collected, the way data are analyzed, and the way the report is written. Therefore, the main purpose of research is to answer a specific research question.

The theory is the mirror of the research. It is a perspective through which the researcher arranges his/her data. The researcher cannot build his/her research in the air. He/she has to build it on the existing data. A theory is an explanation of the existing reality through which the researcher grounds his/her inquiry. In this case, this chapter has provided some criteria for a good theoretical perspective on which the researcher can align his/her collected data.

The strategy of research is the way through which the researcher can present his/her argument. The researcher can decide to present it as deductive or as inductive. However, we have argued in this chapter that deductive strategy is mostly used in presenting quantitative researches and inductive strategy in presenting qualitative researches. In this case, this chapter has also illuminated the researcher towards more complex phenomena of research.

Chapter Highlights

1. A research question is the question that the researcher seeks to answer through collecting firsthand, verifiable and empirical data.

2. The good research question has the following characteristics: it is feasible, has social importance, is relevant, is ethical to participants, and is clear.

3. The research question is important because it guides the literature search, it guides the decision about the kind of research design to employ, it guides

about what data to collect, the analysis of data collected, the writing process, and stops the researcher from going off the truck.

4. The term 'theory' has many definitions. In brief, a theory is an explanation about a social phenomenon that is constantly revised, evaluated and constructed. Theories help to provide a framework of the collected materials. They put the existing knowledge in a particular area in an orderly way.

5. Strategies of research are two: deductive and inductive. Deductive strategy is used when the researcher wants to test a theory in order to confirm or reject it. Inductive strategy is used when the researcher wants to generate a new theory from the collected data.

Study Questions

1. What is a research question? How can you determine a good research question?

2. What is the importance of research questions in doing field researches?

3. Formulate your own research question basing on your own real life situation following all the qualities of a good research question discussed in this chapter.

4. Discuss the meaning of a scientific theory as provided by various writers used in this chapter.

5. Discuss the importance of scientific theory in field research work.

6. How can you determine that a particular theory is useful or useless in your own field research project?

7. Discuss the way in which the two strategies of research, deductive and inductive, work.

8. Discuss the meaning of each of the following terms in research: *hypothesis, variable, independent variable*, and *dependent variable*.

3

The Place of Rules in Academic Research

"There are rules about appropriate content, rules about method and rules about how to behave as a researcher."
—BREW, *THE NATURE OF RESEARCH*, 51

Introduction

IN THE PREVIOUS CHAPTER, we discussed about the relationship between the concepts: research questions, theories, and strategies in research. In this chapter, we will discuss about the place of rules in the execution of academic research. We will start with the importance of rules in conducting research, and then examine the various views on the place of rules in the current context of research. In this case, the chapter will introduce the importance of 'context' in the process of conducting field research.

The Importance of Rules in Research

Academic field research work, its reporting, its dissemination and its evaluation within the academic or scholarly community is based upon a set of rules. Rules play an important role in this case: they are determinants of whether a particular research behavior is acceptable or unacceptable in an academic community, whether a particular theory or method is valid and acceptable, and whether the relationship between knowledge (epistemology) and the nature of reality (ontology) are balanced. In this case, the understanding of a valid research process depends very much on the existing rules of research.[1]

In whatever the case, rules are set to be followed. They are yardsticks that hold reality as being motionless and unchanging. They are boundaries that determine belonging to a research community through governing the acceptability or unacceptability of the works of researchers in the communities they belong. As Angela Brew states it, there are various kinds of rules in the process of research, all aiming at ensuring the quality and acceptability of research work: "There are rules about appropriate content, rules about method and rules about how to behave as a researcher."[2] In that case rules, as Brew quoting Feyerabend (1975) states, "preserve the status quo of intellectual life."[3]

Brew lists 15 rules which have traditionally been followed by academic researchers in the field of education:[4]

1. You must be impartial.

2. You must publish in a refereed journal.

3. You must have lots of references.

4. It must be an academic discourse.

5. No spelling mistakes.

6. You must sound like you have read the book.

7. You must be systematic.

8. You must not intervene in the lives of your 'subjects'.

9. Research must be an original contribution to the field.

10. You must publish.

11. You must be aware of the social and political context.

12. You must be objective.

13. You must find the description of reality/ the 'truth'.

14. You must use an 'acceptable' methodology.

15. You must be detarched.

1. Brew, *The Nature of Research*, 49.
2. Ibid., 51.
3. Ibid.
4. Ibid., 52.

Brew observes that such kinds of rules are not end in themselves. They are not the only determinants of an adequate research in all fields of study. According to Brew these rules

> "form the basis of a self-consistent whole, a coherent system based on a set of assumptions about the nature of reality (ontology) and the nature of knowledge (epistemology). They represent the tradition of inquiry that has been characteristic of Western thought for some considerable time. This tradition enshrines as a view of the nature of reality, assumptions about the logical and empirical requirements for studying it and about the relationship of theories to one another, as well as ideas about the relationship of research findings to reality."[5]

This set of traditionally held rules that characterize the Western thought is known as 'positivism'.[6] Since Auguste Comte coined the term positivism as a unitary set of rules, it has been called in different names by researchers. Brew lists some of these names: "'logical empiricism' (Harré 1981), 'the standard empiricist account' (Hesse 1980), 'the philosophy of knowledge', 'standard empiricism' (Mazwell 1984), 'Enlightenment thinking' (Usher *et al.* 1997), 'conventional inquiry' (Lincoln and Guba 1985), 'objectivism', 'scientific method', 'foundationalism' (Morris 1997), 'modern inquiry' (Mourad 1997) or 'traditional methodology' (Brew 1999)."[7] The main concern of such traditional rules was to control the quality of research in various academic areas according to their contemporary contexts. Traditional rules considered situations as unchanging and rules have to make the research enterprise binding to all researchers in all contexts. In doing that traditional rules for doing and evaluating research fall under a criticism for not taking seriously the changes that happened in various contexts over time, and hence hindering the research's creativity to use context to create new knowledge. The researcher becomes bound to following rules not to exploring the phenomenon on the basis of his/her own understanding.

Rules and the Current Context of Research

The current context of research is considerably different from that of the positivist period. The important question is whether these rules can

5. Ibid., 53.
6. Ibid.
7. Ibid.

remain unchallenged in our own current context. Brew observes that though "the rules of objectivity, consistency, rationality and detarchment" play an important role in judging research and its outcome, yet there have been questions about their efficacy in our ever-changing society.[8] This is partly because research does not only depend on the fixed existing rules in the empiricist framework, but also on a wider range of rules, some emerging within the research process due to the creativity of individual researchers. Research is being freed from the straitjacket of "the consistency of method and content which neatly characterized the positivist philosophy" and its research rules.[9]

"What we are now seeing is a move away from a closed and a coherent (positivist) system of general rules governing research behavior towards open, pluralistic and particularistic systems of rules. These amount to a move towards emphasis on the explanation of how to operate in a complex, uncertain world."[10]

In other words, research becomes known how to do it not only by following the prescribed procedural rules, but also in the process of doing it. Research defines itself in the process of doing it, in the creativity of the researcher within the research process, instead of enclosing the meaning of research within superficial existing traditional rules. The way the researcher determines the idea to research on, the way the researcher turns the idea into a research problem, the way the researcher narrows and defines the research problem formulated, the way the researcher engages into literature reviews to identify the gap of knowledge, the way the researcher designs his/her own research following the existing research paradigms, the way the researcher selects the research instrument for data collection, the way the researcher enters the field, the way the researcher collects data to answer his/her research question, the way the researcher analyzes and interprets the data to hear what informants said, and the way the researcher communicates his/her findings through constructing an informed argument in his/her report, are important processes to provide to the researcher a required definition of research.

However, the above assertion does not, in any way, deny the importance of rules in informing research; and neither does it advocate a research without some kind of rules to ensure its quality. But what is emphasized

8. Ibid., 54.
9. Ibid., 55.
10. Ibid., 55.

is the inefficacy of the empiricist rules in a current complex and dynamic context of research. Brew prefers the word 'guidelines' instead of 'rules'.[11] In this complex and dynamic context of research, rules are mostly 'guidelines' to ensure the quality of research instead of being fixed formulas which without being followed research cannot be valid. Brew, using the work of C.E. Glassick, M. T. Huber and G. I. Maeroff (1997), lists six new rules (guidelines) used by university promotion committees, granting agents, scholarly journals, university press and teaching evaluation in the U.S. for the work that is academically sound. These guidelines are the following:

1. Clear goals, well defined, significant and feasible.

2. Adequate up-to-date preparation with a clear understanding and capacity to realize the goals, i.e. competence of the staff carrying the work.

3. Choice of appropriate methods

4. Significance of the results: that what has been accomplished adds something to the field.

5. Effective communication: sharing scholarly work with others (including teaching) with a plan for reporting and dissemination.

6. Accompanied by reflective critique in which one's own learning is developed, i.e. learning to do it better.[12]

What Brew suggests above is the new, fragile context of research we have in the postmodern era.[13] Brew contents that since context changes, there is a little need for fixed rules to govern the ways to conduct and evaluate research because they can easily prove irrelevant. She is in a position to suggest for the construction of guidelines that can govern research in regard to contexts and types of research to be conducted. In the following chapter, we will indulge ourselves into a more detail on the nature of fieldwork and its characteristics as qualitative research.

11. Ibid., 57.

12. Ibid.

13. We will discuss the concept of post-modernism and its features further in chapter five below.

Conclusion

In this chapter we have addressed the question of rules in academic research. Given the context of research we have now (the postmodern context) the chapter has examined the various views on the place of rules in research. This chapter has vividly shown that rules of research can now best work as guidelines to lead researchers into wise decisions on what should be the appropriate conduct. Therefore, this chapter subjects the reader into a thoughtful examination of rules that were dearly held by modern researchers as being the determinants of valid research.

Chapter Highlights

1. Rules of Research are yardsticks that hold reality as being motionless and unchanging. They are boundaries that determine belonging to a research community. It governs the acceptability or unacceptability of the works of researchers in the communities they belong.

2. The current context of research is different from that of the positivist period. This means that research is being freed from the straitjacket of having a consistence of method and content, which were the sole characters of the positivist philosophy.

3. In this postmodern era, rules for research can best work as guidelines to lead researchers into wise decisions on what should be the appropriate conduct.

Study Questions

1. What does it mean to say that rules of research in the postmodern era are mostly guidelines?

2. Suppose there were no rules guiding the way to conduct research, how would the research process look line? Discuss this question in a more detail.

3. Evaluate the various views about rules of research discussed in this chapter. What is your own opinion regarding those views?

4

Fieldwork as Qualitative Research

"Qualitative fieldwork is a process whereby "some person (a social science researcher) collaborates with another person (variously called subject, respondent or informant) to create a social relationship within which an exchange of information occurs."

—AGAR, *THE PROFESSIONAL STRANGER*, 1

Introduction

NORMALLY THE WORD 'FIELDWORK' has been loosely understood to refer to agricultural work performed by hand in a particular area. However, researchers have found that the meaning of the word has been changing to mean "the act of inquiring into the nature of phenomena by studying them at first hand in the environments in which they naturally exist or occur."[1] In this case, instead of using soil or ground as a place for fieldwork, fieldworkers use human beings as subjects of their investigations with the purpose of obtaining firsthand information about their questions or problems.

Robert A. Georges and Michael O. Jones further write: "Long associated with the activities of the folklorist, anthropologist, linguist, and sociologist, fieldwork now attracts the psychologist, artist, ethnomusicologist, educator, historian, and student of dance and theatre. Courses

1. Georges & Jones, *The Human Element*, 1.

38

in fieldwork have proliferated in colleges and universities, and they are often an integral part of transforming programs for military and law enforcement personnel."[2]

What Georges and Jones present above is the wide spreading use of the word 'fieldwork' in various areas of study or work. This means that facts are not studied only in the classrooms, but also in real areas where people live and interact. If students are provided a chance to visit a coffee processing industry, a tea processing industry, a farm, or a poultry project, they will have a chance to gain knowledge from what is going on in those areas. This kind of knowledge is called 'empirical knowledge'. It is knowledge gained from the real situation. Therefore, students pay only one visit to an area; but, the knowledge they get remain in their memories for a long period of time.

What Is Fieldwork?

Fieldwork is a study that uses scientific ways to study what goes on in the environment. It is a result of relationship between the researcher and the people or objects in that environment. Michael H. Agar defines fieldwork as a process of human relationship. For Agar, fieldwork is a process whereby "some person (a social science researcher) collaborates with another person (variously called *subject, respondent* or *informant*) to create a social relationship within which an exchange of information occurs."[3] In this case, a field researcher studies the ordinary activities of the people in a particular setting by interacting face-to-face with environments of study with the aim of understanding what they mean to people who undergo them in that particular environment.

Since science uses the laboratory to discover or make theories about phenomena, fieldwork uses environment and people within it as its laboratory to make discoveries and construct theories about existing phenomena. Field researchers study the activities in the setting through interacting, listening, asking questions, and observing what people are doing in their daily routines. Field research is a study in the naturalistic setting of activities carried out by people. The researcher has to leave the office and interact with people in their naturalistic setting, live their lives, eat what they eat, participate and observe what they do and think about them. In this way, fieldwork enables students to be independent discoverers because it allows them to reach the

2. Ibid.
3. Agar, *The Professional Stranger*, 1.

39

real world and use their own minds to discern what is going on there. For these students, the environment and its people becomes their source of information for acquiring knowledge as the laboratory work is.

The knowledge gained from fieldwork is different from the one gained in classrooms. The classroom knowledge is mostly theoretical based on the teacher as the provider, or based on one's reading of written materials. Classroom knowledge is in most cases hard to comprehend and easy to forget. Knowledge gained from fieldwork is knowledge through ones eyes and ears. Sometimes it involves one's hands and legs. The fieldworker has to see what goes on and to hear what is said. In order to hear and see, the researcher has to go to the real places and sometimes participate in what goes on. Therefore, what is perceived through the fieldworker's seeing, hearing or participating lasts for a long time in his/her memory as compared to what the fieldworker hears from the teacher in the classroom or reads in written materials.

Types of Fieldwork

The word 'fieldwork' is broad. It implies several activities depending on the interests of the fieldworker; but, all of them aim at providing him/her with some facts about the world. Two of these types include: excursion and field research. To do an excursion is to hold a trip, a visit to a particular place for the purpose of learning. Students can visit an industry, a school or farm. This is sometimes called study tour. The main aim of such study tour is to reinforce what students learned theoretically in classes. Through the study tour conducted, students make connections of what they learned theoretically in class, and what they see in the real situation. In excursions, students can get a chance to converse with some people in the areas and observe what goes on. Hence they can write useful notes which can help them remember what they saw and heard.

Field Research is much broader. It is an advanced way of fieldwork which deals with a particular problem. The field researcher engages in research in order to find answers for the problem at hand. In this type of fieldwork, the researcher uses advanced ways of collecting data in order to prove or disprove a hypothesis, or provides explanations (theory) about an existing phenomenon. In order to do this, the researcher needs to identify a problem, see what other people have done with the problem, design his/her research, collect data, analyze and interpret those data, and eventually present it for the wider readership. In other words, field research is a rigorous type of fieldwork. Hence in this book we will mainly be concerned with this type of fieldwork.

Importance of Fieldwork

Paul K. Kibuuka and Robert Karuggah outline the importance of field-work.[4] For them, fieldwork is important for several aspects. Some of these aspects are the following: First, fieldwork is important because it is a tool for self-teaching. The teacher is less involved in the fieldwork. Students themselves interact with the real world to understand it for themselves. In being observant and hearing what is talked, they learn for themselves to select relevant information which will lead them to drawing useful conclusion basing on what they observed and heard from the field.

Second, fieldwork is important because it provides fieldworkers with skills about collecting, analyzing, and presenting the analyzed and interpreted data. In doing this, fieldworkers increase their ability to reason logically and present their reasoning accurately while making their own independent judgments on what they present.

Third, for students, fieldwork enhances a good correlation between what they theoretically learn in the class and what is real in the world around them. The natural setting and explanations obtained from the field become great teachers despite the teachers in classrooms and the written documents they read. Therefore, this way of learning enables students to apply the knowledge gained in classrooms to the real life situations.

Fourth, classroom teaching is in most cases monotonous. Fieldwork helps break monotony. Students lose attention if they always listen to the same teacher with the same style of teaching, the same voice. An opportunity to have fieldwork enables them to change learning environments and voices. In exchanging environments, students create in their minds critical thinking because they start themselves making sense of the world around them instead of listening to the teacher.

Fifth, fieldwork is important because it is the main source of getting primary data. Researchers or fieldworkers need to get this information in order to understand people's lived-experiences from the real situation. Hence fieldwork becomes an important part of qualitative research because it deals with firsthand information from the real lived-experiences of the real situations.

4. Kibuuka & Karuggah, *Certificate Geography*, 92–93.

Field Research as Qualitative Research

Having defined fieldwork, mentioned its types, and stated its importance, we now turn to looking at field research as a qualitative research. Since this book is mainly based on the ways of doing qualitative research, this chapter, and the following chapters, will devote themselves more on dealing with qualitative field research and its features. As the name implies, field research as qualitative research emphasizes on the "quality" of social phenomena, social situations, or social issues. Hence, field research as qualitative research seeks to understand and provide explanations on the meaning of social issues, phenomena or situations within a particular society as understood and practiced by the members of that society.

Since qualitative research seeks to explore the 'meaning' of social phenomena, issues, or situations as understood by members of that society, it is commonly referred to as being interpretive, naturalistic, field, participant observation, inductive, case study or ethnographic research.[5] These terminologies imply that in qualitative research, knowledge about a particular phenomenon, issues or situation is embedded in people's lived-experiences and can be explored and uncovered by the inquiring initiative of the researcher. So each of the terminologies above indicates that there is an interaction between people who have a particular 'lived-experience' about the phenomenon, issue, or situation being studied and the researcher who rigorously aspires to uncover the embedded knowledge through his/her perception.[6]

Features of Qualitative Research

Before entering into a detailed discussion of qualitative field research, it is important that we look at the distinction between qualitative and quantitative researches. How can we distinguish qualitative research from quantitative research? There is a difference between qualitative and quantitative researches as types of research inquiry. While quantitative research emphasizes on the measurement of the 'parts' of a particular phenomenon, issue, or situation, i.e., its component parts (variables), qualitative research examines the whole phenomenon, issue or situation. Qualitative research is not interested in the measurement of the *relationship between variables*, but in *the meaning of the whole social phenomenon or issue* under investigation

5. Merriam, *Qualitative Research*, 5.
6. Ibid., 6.

as lived and understood by people in a particular social group. Merriam puts it so clearly: "Qualitative researchers *are interested in understanding the meaning people have constructed*, that is, how they make sense of their world and the experiences they have in the world."[7] While quoting Sherman and Webb Merriam adds: "Qualitative research 'implies a direct concern with experience as it is 'lived' or 'felt' or undergone.'"[8] According to Merriam, therefore, the main philosophical assumption that underlies all qualitative researches "is the view that reality is constructed by individuals interacting with their social worlds."[9] In short, therefore, Newman and Benz write: "The qualitative, naturalistic approach is used when observing and interpreting reality with the aim of developing a theory that will explain what was experienced. The quantitative approach is used when one begins with a theory (or hypothesis) and tests for confirmation or disconfirmation of that hypothesis."[10] In this case, as Gall, Borg and Gall describe it: "qualitative research is best used to discover themes and relationships at the case level, while quantitative research is best used to validate those themes and relationships in samples and populations. (. . .) qualitative research plays a discovery role, while quantitative research plays a confirmatory role."[11]

Following the above description of qualitative and quantitative researches, let us analyze, in a more detail, some of the characteristics of qualitative field research drawing from Merriam. Merriam lists the following characteristics of qualitative field researches that more clearly distinguish it from quantitative field research:[12] First, qualitative field research seeks to understand phenomena, issues or situations from the perspective, or viewpoint of those participating in the research process, those whom the researcher explores the phenomenon (participants), and not from the perspective of the researcher. In such way, qualitative research understands phenomena in the "insider's" perspective (emic perspective) and not from the "outsider's" perspective (etic perspective). Insiders here are the participants who have a 'lived'-experience of the phenomenon under study; and outsiders are the researchers who are not part of those experiencing the phenomenon under study.

7. Ibid (emphasis is in original).

8. Ibid.

9. Ibid.

10. Newman & Benz, *Qualitative-Quantitative*, 3.

11. Gall, Borg & Gall, *Educational Research*, 29.

12. Merriam, *Qualitative Research*, 7–8.

Second, in qualitative field research "the researcher is the primary instrument for data collection and analysis."[13] This means that whatever instrument used in collecting qualitative data, it is secondary to the researcher's perception. The researcher stands primary in the data mediating process.

Third, qualitative field research *usually involves fieldwork. The researcher must physically go to the people, setting, site, institution (the field) in order to observe behaviour in its natural setting.*"[14] However, it is not necessary that all qualitative studies should involve the researcher going to the field. Occasionally, researchers can analyze available data from documents, photographs, inscriptions, etc., to ascertain meaning as understood by the concerned owner of such material. However, any called field research involves going to natural settings of phenomena.

The fourth characteristic of qualitative field research has to do with the strategy of inquiry it uses. This type of research *"employs an inductive research strategy."*[15] This means that the logic of the research is meant to generate, or build up concepts, hypotheses, and theories from the collected data. Its aim is not to test the existing theory by examining the relationship between particular variables or concepts of a phenomenon (as quantitative research does). Merriam thus emphasizes: "Often qualitative studies are undertaken because there is a lack of theory, or existing theory fails to explain a phenomenon. (. . .). Qualitative researchers build toward theory from observations and intuitive understandings gained in the field."[16] Merriam, quoting Goetz and LeCompte, further adds: "In contrast to deductive [or quantitative] researchers who 'hope to find data to match a theory,' inductive [or qualitative] researchers hope to find a theory that explains their data.' Typically, qualitative research findings are in the form of themes, categories, typologies, concepts, tentative hypotheses, even theory which have been inductively derived from the data."[17] Being inductive in its strategy of inquiry, qualitative research makes data the main source of where new theories can be generated to explain social phenomena.

The fifth characteristic of qualitative field research has to do with the product or the nature of the outcome. Merriam argues that "since qualitative research focuses on process, meaning, and understanding, *the product*

13. Ibid., 7.
14. Ibid.
15. Ibid.
16. Ibid.
17. Ibid., 7–8.

of qualitative study is richly descriptive. Words and pictures rather than numbers are used to convey what the researcher has learned about a phenomenon. (. . .). In addition, data in the form of participants' own words, direct citations from documents, excerpts of videotapes, and so on, are likely to be included to support the findings of the study."[18]

The question is what does qualitative field research specifically focus on? Chamblis and Schutt list seven aspects which qualitative field research is much more concerned about:

> A focus on meanings rather than on quantifiable phenomena.
>
> Collection of much data on a few cases rather than little data on many cases.
>
> Study in depth and detail, without predetermined categories or directions, rather than emphasis on analyses and categories determined in advance.
>
> Conception of the researcher as an 'instrument,' rather than as the designer of objective instruments to measure particular variables.
>
> Sensitivity to context, rather than seeking universal generalizations.
>
> Attention to the impact of the researcher's and other's values on the course of the analysis, rather than presuming the possibility of value-free inquiry.
>
> A goal of rich descriptions of the world rather than measurement of specific variables.[19]

Therefore, qualitative field research helps us understand some important aspects such as: the meaning of the phenomenon for participants in the studied area, the context within which participants experience the phenomenon together with the influence which this context has to the existence of the phenomenon, the unanticipated influences brought about by the phenomenon which lead the researcher to modifying the study in the course of the process, and the process through which the phenomenon takes place. The process by which events and actions take place in a particular area of research is the main interest of qualitative field research.

Eventually, qualitative field research should develop explanations (theory). This is what Miles and Huberman state regarding qualitative field research when they write: "Much resent research supports the claim that we wish to make there: that field research is far *better* than sorely quantified

18. Ibid., 8.

19. Chamblis & Schutt, *Making Sense*, 196–97.

approaches at developing explanations of what we call local causality—the actual events and processes that led to specific customs."[20] Therefore, qualitative field research becomes a step-by-step process which leads us towards understanding the above aspects.

Steps We Expect to See in Qualitative Field Research

The researcher should bear in mind that one of the important aspects in any qualitative research is *quality*. The quality tells the reader something about the process of research and the capability of the researcher. According to Locke, Silverman & Spirduso we expect to see the following steps in a qualitative field research:[21] First, the purpose and general rationale of the study. This step responds to two questions 'what' and 'why'. The 'what' question explores the problem selected, and the 'why' question explores the importance or significance or worthiness of the problem. In responding to the above questions, the researcher explains what was the general purpose of his/her study, and how did that researcher make a case for the general importance of the study to himself, to the researched community and to the academic community.

The second aspect concerns the fit and specific rationale. The main concern of the second step is to answer the question 'where'. As Pazmiño points out: "The question considers where one locates a particular work in the universe of possibilities and in relation to the work of others."[22] This means that the researcher has to describe the way in which the topic researched fits into the existing research literature and how such fitting provides evidence that a new research needs to be conducted. In this case, the researcher has to conduct adequate literature review and identify a gap of knowledge about the phenomenon before embarking in any field research.

The main concerns of the third, fourth, fifth, sixth, and seventh steps are to answer the question 'how'. Answering the question 'how' means describing the methods of inquiry employed in the study and the methodological aspects involved in the study. Therefore, the third step concerns about research participants. Here the researcher should introduce himself/herself as the primary participant and a tool for data collection. The researcher also introduces the relationship he/she had with the purpose of

20. Miles & Huberman, *Qualitative Data*, 132.

21. Locke, Silverman & Spirduso, *Reading and Understanding*, 103–9.

22. Pazmiño, *Doing Theological Research*, 20.

the research, with the rest of the research participants and the research area. The researcher needs to provide a description of who was studied and why. Here the number of participants and their categories need to be provided.

The fourth step concerns the context of research. Here the researcher needs to describe the area where the research took place, the important characteristics of that area and the way such characteristics suited the study undertaken. It should be clearly understood that context is central to qualitative fieldwork. Therefore, the descriptions of what was going on in the research area are important to justify the importance of the research just carried out.

The fifth concerns steps in sequence. Here the researcher describes the main procedural steps that were used in the study in order to reach the goal. The researcher needs to outline the way he/she started his/her study, how the study was designed and carried out, what instruments were used for data collection and why use such instruments. Therefore, this place will outline all methods involved in conducting the field study.

The sixth concerns data and data collection. Here the researcher describes what type of data did he/she collect? Were they secondary or primary data? Were they field notes, interview scripts, photographs, diary notes or audio records? Were they from books, journals, meetings or monographs? Why he/she decided to collect the data of that type?

The seventh concerns the analysis and interpretation of that data. Here the researcher describes what form of data analysis was used. Is it content analysis, or any other? Why did he use such type of data analysis? How did he/she go about making sense of that data?

The following two last steps respond to the question 'who' or 'for whom'. The question explores the audience for which research report is communicated, and in what way the research report is communicated for the maximum understanding of that particular audience. Therefore the eighth step concerns about the communication of research findings. Here the researcher identifies the main findings of his/her study. He/she tells what was going on in his/her research area during the time the research was conducted. The researcher tells this in a clear and understandable language. It is here that the researcher interprets what he/she got from the research in order to hear what the respondents meant in what they said. His/her interpretation bases on the themes obtained from the analysis process.

The ninth step concerns about the study conclusion. Here the researcher states three important aspects: the way his/her results responded to the purpose of the research, his/her recommendations on steps to be taken in order to deal with the research problem, and his/her recommendations and suggestions for further qualitative field study. In providing his/her recommendations for further research, the research has to suggest the areas which need further investigations.

Conclusion

The main concern of the book is doing qualitative field research. This chapter began to incorporate the reader into this core concern of the book. The chapter defined fieldwork, stated the types of fieldwork, and the importance of fieldwork. Through the description of features of qualitative research, the chapter has demonstrated the importance of this kind of research. The chapter ended up with the description of the various steps to be followed in conducting qualitative field researches. This chapter is important because it shows that field research is the type of research whose main foundation is the interaction with participants in order to generate new understandings about taken for granted phenomena within societies.

Chapter Highlights

1. Fieldwork is a study that uses scientific ways to study what goes on in the environment. It is a result of relationship between the researcher and the people or objects in that environment.

2. Instead of using the laboratory, as natural scientists do, fieldwork studies the activities in the natural setting through interacting, listening, asking questions, and observing what people are doing in their daily routines.

3. Field research is important in several aspects: First, it is a self-teaching process; second, it provides fieldworkers with skills about collecting, analyzing, and presenting the analyzed and interpreted data; third, it provides a good correlation from what is studied in class and what is studied in the field; fourth, it helps break monotony experienced from classroom teaching; fifth, it helps the researcher obtain primary data.

4. Qualitative research emphasizes on 'quality', not 'quantity' of social phenomena, social situations, or social issues. Qualitative research studies phenomena in the 'insider's' perspective (etic perspective) not in the 'outsider's' perspective (emic perspective).

5. In this case, field research, as qualitative research, has its foundation in the interaction with participants in order to generate new understanding about taken for granted phenomena.

Study Questions

1. If you are planning to conduct field research, it is likely that you will provide a brief description of field research in your proposal. Discuss as much as you can what does it mean by field research. What are the types of field researches?

2. What qualifies field research as being qualitative research?

3. By using as many other literatures as possible discuss the features that distinguish qualitative field research from quantitative field research.

4. List the steps we expect to see in a qualitative field research as stated in this chapter and discuss each step in a more detail basing on the context of your own field of study.

5

Identifying the Research Problem

"A research problem (. . .) can be anything that a person finds un-satisfactory or unsettling, a difficulty of some sort, a state of affairs that needs to be changed, anything that is not working as well as it might. Problems involve areas of concern to researchers, conditions they want to improve, difficulties they want to eliminate, questions for which they seek answers."

—FRAENKEL, WALLEN & HYUN, *HOW TO DESIGN*, 27.

Introduction

AFTER DISCUSSING ABOUT THE nature of fieldwork, its distinguishing features as qualitative research, and its expected steps, we now start exploring the 'what' and 'why' questions of the research steps outlined in the previous chapter. We now turn to looking more closely at the way the researcher can identify the problem for his/her research purpose. We will discuss about the researcher's responsibility to conduct a reconnaissance, to select the problem to research on, to narrow it down and to define it more clearly. Therefore, this chapter provides the researcher some important clues to follow in order to have a well refined and rational research problem before engaging oneself into a research proper.

Conducting a Reconnaissance

Before conducting a research on anything, the researcher needs to know what issue or subject he/she is interested to study. In order to know what issue or subject to research on, the researcher needs to conduct a reconnaissance. Reconnaissance is a pre-visit to the research area before the real research is conducted. The *researcher* pays this visit with a special purpose. Reconnaissance is important for researchers in the following aspects: First, it helps him/her to collect general information which will help formulate relevant research problem and research questions depending on the type of people and the situation of the area. It becomes difficult for the researcher entering the field for the first time to know what to ask and who to ask. Entering the field before the real research helps the researcher to make some arrangements and to know the way to go about with his/her research process.

Reconnaissance helps the researcher to determine the appropriate method to use in his/her research. The method to use in collecting data depends sorely on the type of people and the situation of the area. Not all methods are suitable for all people in all times and at all situations. Methods are context sensitive. The method which is suitable in one place is not necessarily suitable in another. Therefore, the visit to the research area before the real research helps the researcher to determine the appropriate method which will help him/her to be efficient in the research process.

One of the characteristics of fieldwork is that it is time consuming. The fieldworker has to use his/her time in the field. Since fieldwork takes time, the researcher needs to organize the way he/she can minimize time in whatever means possible. His/her visit to the research area before the research proper will enable him/her to organize it in such a way that he/she will save time when conducting the research.

Conducting fieldwork is also costly. It is difficult to estimate the actual costs required without knowing the research area beforehand. Reconnaissance is important because it will enable the researcher to know the real situation of the area of study, and hence estimate the costs required. Reconnaissance also helps the researcher to plan the way to start and the way to end up the research process. In this case, we can say that through a prior visit to the research area, the researcher can select an appropriate problem grounded from the research area, ask relevant questions regarding the problem of research, and plan his/her fieldwork schedule more accurately.

Selecting the Research Problem or Question

There is a common belief among most researchers that the primary purpose of doing research is to prove the validity of the pre-conceived assumptions or hypotheses about the existing phenomenon. This belief is in most cases erroneous.[1] "Rather, research," according to Brause, "is a process of searching repeatedly, *re*-searching for new insights and a more comprehensive, cohesive, 'elegant' theory. (. . .). Each research project intends to advance our knowledge, getting closer to the 'truth' (. . .). Findings from research allow us to make potentially more accurate predictions."[2] In this case, a choice of a better research problem, topic or question to study is important in order to provide new insights in a particular field of study.

According to Ndunguru "A statement of a research problem then constitutes *what is it that we don't know or understand about its workings, causes, effects, or future behavior for the given social phenomenon?*"[3] Fraenkel, Wallen & Hyun also define statement of the problem thus: "A research problem (. . .) can be anything that a person finds unsatisfactory or unsettling, a difficulty of some sort, a state of affairs that needs to be changed, anything that is not working as well as it might. Problems involve areas of concern to researchers, conditions they want to improve, difficulties they want to eliminate, questions for which they seek answers."[4]

Some Guidelines for Selecting Topics or Problems

Following the above definitions of a research problem, Johann Mouton provides us some guidelines on selecting a suitable research topic or problem. We list and discuss these guidelines below:

1. "Select a topic [or research problem] that is relevant to your own short-term career prospects, whether it be a career in research or any other profession."[5]

According to the above guideline, the important thing to consider is one's career. The topic should fit into one's career. Even though the research is done in a short-term basis, it needs to continue sounding in the career

1. Brause, *Writing Your Doctoral Dissertation*, 37.
2. Ibid.
3. Ndunguru, *Lectures on Research*, 35 (emphasis is in original).
4. Fraenkel, Wallen & Hyun, *How to Design*, 27.
5. Mouton, *How to Succeed*, 39.

of the researcher. In order for it to continue sounding, the interest of the researcher in a particular topic is important. The topic needs to maintain the interest of the researcher. It should not make the researcher regret on what was done during his/her research after duration of time has lapsed.

2. *"Select a topic [or research problem] that you find intellectually stimulating and that you are convinced will sustain your interest for a number of years."*[6]

According to the above guideline, what counts a lot in the suitability of a particular topic is its ability to make the researcher anxious to continue inquiring about the issue it addresses. In other words, the topic needs to be an ever-stimulating and attractive to the researcher. It can be agreed, however, that the topic cannot be interesting to everybody. The topic is interesting to the researcher and his/her own personal interests. Hence, selecting a topic that maintains the researcher's interest for a long time makes the topic selected to be alive in the life and duties of the researcher.

The main obstacles of selecting a topic that is interesting and stimulating to the researcher are the constraints of the funding agents and faculties where the research is to be submitted after its completion. Funding agents and faculties or research programs may need particular topics, related to certain issues of their own interests in order to be accepted for funding. In that situation researchers may be bound to follow the constraints of the agents instead of following their own interests.

In whatever the case, the researcher needs to remember that a topic selected out of his/her interests loses its credibility in the course of the researcher's life. It also loses the researcher's ambition to continue inquiring about it, and eventually faces a natural death. This is, in most cases, what happens to researches that are carried under certain constraints and restrictions.

3. *"Select a topic [or research problem] that is researchable in the sense that you will be able not only merely complete it with the available resources, but also complete it at a level of scholarship that is scientifically acceptable."*[7]

According to Mouton, researchability of a particular topic means its ability to be researched and completed successfully within the allocated time-span and by the use of the available resources in that particular time.[8] When Mouton speaks of the researchability of the topic, he also touches

6. Ibid., 40 cf. the tips in Machi & McEvoy, *The Literature Review*, 10.

7. Mouton, *How to Succeed*, 40.

8. Ibid.

issues of the narrowness of the topic. If the topic is broad, it is possible that its researchability is limited. The narrower the topic the greater is its researchability. This is mainly because the researcher will have to deal with very few issues in a particular topic. If the topic is broad, the researcher will fail to handle all issues related to the topic at a given period. Hence, instead of attempting to research at a topic that is complicated and difficult to complete within a particular time-frame, the researcher needs to consider narrowing his/her topic towards a more precise and manageable one.

4. "Select the topic [or research problem] that you find interesting and worthwhile. Then read more about it and focus more narrowly, delineating it into a more specific topic. After you have done this, think again about how you can make it more specific and researchable. Repeat this process until you and your supervisor are convinced that you have sufficiently focused the research topic!"[9]

The underlying demand posed by the above guideline is the focusing of the topic towards a particular issue to be studied. Focusing needs thinking and re-thinking around the topic. The researcher needs to limit himself/herself into what he/she thinks to be the most worthwhile of all. The researcher also needs to be convinced that he/she has exhausted most of the needed effort towards a specific issue to be researched. The researcher also needs to convince his/her supervisor that what has been specified in the topic is worthwhile, researchable, and comes from the researcher's own efforts.

Select the Topic Which Is Important

According to my view, one of the important questions to ask oneself in selecting a topic for research is the following: Is this topic important and worth studying? This question leads the researcher towards answering the question 'why'. It leads to exploring the rationale of the selected topic. It is not enough to have an interesting topic; the topic needs to be important to the researcher, to the participants of the research, and possibly to the community at large. As the researcher sets on to select a topic for a particular research project, the researcher needs to ask oneself the following questions: "Why is this topic important? To whom would it be important? How could the results be used? What are the broader concerns of which this research is part?"[10]

9. Ibid.

10. Rubin & Rubin, *Qualitative Interviewing*, 52.

Herbert J. Rubin and Irine S. Rubin suggest some issues that contribute to the selected topic being important and worth studying. First, the topic is important if it makes open and makes clear a problem that has been invisible in a particular society or group of study for so long. Sometimes the problem may be invisible because it has been silenced, or people experiencing such a problem have been voiceless. If the topic provides voice to the voiceless people, it should be considered important, both to the researcher and to the community of people experiencing such a problem.[11]

If the researcher sets on to study the phenomenon of stigmatization of PLWHA in the society, the abuse of children, the killing of people with skin impairment (people with albinism), the mistreatment of wives by their husbands at homes, etc, these should be considered important topics because such studies long to uncover hidden reasons for the persistence of such undesirable phenomena. In that case, the study contributes not only to the understanding of the researcher, but also of the people experiencing the problem and the society at large.[12]

Second, according to Rubin and Rubin, the topic chosen is important if it serves to clarify the visible problem but not well-understood by people experiencing it, or by the community at large.[13] If the topic concerns, for example, with alcoholism, drug abuse, etc, aspects which people see them as problems, but do not understand the extend to which the above-mentioned activities as being problematic. The study to clarify the understanding of the problem among such activities should be considered important.

Third, the topic is important if it deals with a problem whose solution is far beyond the existing understanding of people, or if it addresses an existing dilemma regarding a particular issue. For example, HIV infection and AIDS are current unsolvable problems. People are infected by HIV and eventually develop AIDS. The cure for AIDS and the vaccine for HIV are current problems. If the topic is chosen to address why HIV and AIDS are still persistent in communities, that kind of topic should be considered important.

Fourth, the topic is genuine if it indicates a particular cause that brings a considerable effect in the life of a particular community. Such cause may include, for example, the increase in taxes to small scale business people, the emergence of gun-ridden theft in public banks, etc. Such topics that

11. Ibid.
12. Ibid.
13. Ibid.

address a particular cause seeming to have a considerable effect in the life of the society are important topics.[14]

Fifth, the topic is important if it attempts to resolve a particular existing dilemma in the life of a particular group of people. Such dilemmas that can be addressed include: the use of condoms—should people use them to protect themselves against HIV infection, or respect the values embraced by their religious teachings? Female circumcision is another example of such dilemmas—should people continue with their traditional practices of circumcising women or adhere to anti-Female Genital Mutilation programs? Topics addressing such and related issues can be considered important for the researcher and the community wrestling with them.

Sixth, the topic is important if the problem it purports is not limited to a particular location where research is done. The research area should be a sample area of study whose findings can have implications in other places. For example, the question of stigmatization of People living with HIV/AIDS, the question of street children, the question of drug use, the question of alcoholism, and many others, are not located only in a particular location. They are persistent problems in almost everywhere. What differs greatly is the context of their appearance. In this case, findings of topics addressing such problems are not significant to the places where they occur, but can be relevant to other contexts with similar problems.[15]

The Various Places to Get Adequate Topics for Research

Where will the researcher get an important topic to study? The first place to get a research topic is from course works that the student undergoes or the researcher conducts. It is also possible to get a topic out of the course-work, but the most important thing in obtaining a good title is primarily determined by one's 'readiness' to launch the research process. When the student or researcher is ready for the process of research the signs of readiness will be vivid leading the student or researcher to identify the issue for study more easily. Brause lists several aspects that indicate personal readiness for a researcher to identify a research topic or question for study: "a sense of wonder, interest, and/or excitement about a specific topic or question; extensive familiarity with 'the literature' and the current state of knowledge in the field of discipline (. . .); encouragement and support for

14. Ibid., 53.
15. Cf. Ibid.

you and your ideas within your program community; time to work on the project; a desire to contribute to a discipline or field; and a determination to complete the [research project] (. . .)."[16] Identifying a good topic, problem, or question for study depends greatly on the above-mentioned aspects. Therefore the researcher is the main determinant of his/her own research to be conducted: the way the researcher perceives of the problem, the way he/she is anxious to contribute to knowledge, and the way the researcher is convinced that it is possible for him/her to pursue the research task.

The most important issues to considers in identifying a topic or question for study are two: How far is the issue to be studied practical, and how far is it interesting to the researcher himself/herself. The practicality of the research topic or question for study implies the workability of that topic or question within the prescribed time frame, and the possibility to obtain adequate sources for that particular topic or question. The topic that is practical should also be interesting and exiting to the researcher. An interesting topic will keep the researcher motivated to continue throughout the prescribed time without loosing courage to continue.

The intriguing question is on how to obtain such a topic. Brause provides some options of places one can obtain such a topic or question:

- You draw from the knowledge which you acquired in your coursework and from your independent reading and journal writing.

- You engage in dialogues with professors about topics which might be acceptable, knowing your [project] will only get done with the assistance and support of the faculty [or community of researchers].

- You collaborate with student-colleagues, discussing the topics they are contemplating for their researches (. . .).

- You draw on your personal and professional experiences.[17]

In all the above endeavors the researcher is trying to do what Bernard C. Beins and Agatha M. Beins call the 'pre-research' process. However, in order to obtain a clearly focused title for study several stages must be accomplished. These stages aim at providing the researcher with important information which will eventually lead him/her towards formulating a logical and more useful problem for his/her research. Kumar states: "A research problem

16. Brause, *Writing your Doctoral Dissertation*, 38.
17. Ibid., 48.

identifies your destination: It should tell you, your research advisor and your readers *what* you intend to research."[18] It needs to be well-thought, well-formulated, precise, specific and clear. This is because almost everything that follows in the research process is dependant upon the problem formulated.

Components of a Good Research Topic or Problem

In order for the problem or topic selected to be promising and worthwhile, it needs to answer the following rhetorical questions: *what* is really intended to be researched by using this title or problem selected, *how* will the researcher go about researching the topic or problem, *whom* (*which* context or population) does the researcher intends to research. Look at the following example of a title of one of my books:

> *Jesus and the Divorce Commandment: Reading the Gospel of Mark in a Context of Divorce and Remmariage in Tanzania*

In the above example, the main title "*Jesus and the Divorce Commandment*" states the *what* of the title. It describes the content of the research. The wards "*Reading the Gospel of Mark*" describe the *how* of the research. It is a hermeneutical reading of Mark. The words indicate the methodology to be employed in the research process. The words "*in a context of Divorce and Remarriage in Tanzania*" describe the context and population of research. It is a Tanzanian context and population. In this case, the title is self explanatory in terms of the content of research expected, the methodology to be used in the research, and the context and population of research.

Narrowing the Problem

In the book *Quality Research Papers*, Vyhmeister states: "Once you have selected a topic, you must identify the problem or issue to be tackled. The issue must be specific, often expressed as a research question, not something vague and general."[19] As I stated in the above paragraph, you need to answer the question "what" more clearly. In order to get a specific issue to deal with, the researcher needs to narrow down the broad topic selected into one specific aspect. It is common among both students and experienced

---

18. Kumar, *Research Methodology*, 20.

19. Vyhmeister, *Quality Research Papers*, 3, cf. Ndunguru, *Lectures on Research*, 36.

researchers to embark on broad research topics or problems, sometimes unknowingly. This is because it needs to be careful to work with a topic in order to have it as narrow as possible. Narrowing the research problem or topic means focusing the research into its few manageable aspects according to the time limit available. The broad text usually leads to superficial research work and even re-production of what has already been researched by other researchers. A good research project needs a narrowed focus in order for it to be meaningful and manageable.

The problem with narrowing the research topic is to know whether the research topic has been narrowed enough for one's research purpose. The following are some of the hints that can enable the researcher to know that the topic or problem needs further narrowing. First, availability of plenty of literature at the shelf of books that are published about the topic and that could function as references for the topic. This shows that the topic is not focused enough into a specific problem that needs to be studied by the researcher. Second, topics that can be summed up by ONE or TWO words are, in most cases, broad. Topics such as 'theology', 'systematic theology', 'physical geography', 'sociology', 'literature', etc., are still too broad to be research topics. Third, one should find easy to formulate a thesis statement from the research topic because it has few manageable aspects. If the researcher finds it difficult to formulate this statement, it suggests that the topic still has many aspects that need to be dropped down in order to be focused.

Defining the Problem

After shortly describing the way the researcher should narrow his/her problem, we now turn towards defining the narrowed problem. What does exactly mean by defining the problem? Since research in its broader sense is based upon a particular problem, the problem needs to be *clear, concise, focused*, and *convincing* to the researcher himself/herself and to other people who come across it. In order for it to have these qualities, it needs some explanations from the researcher's point of view. In brief, we can say that defining the problem for research is stating it in the view of its boundaries. Therefore, defining a research problem "involves the task of laying down boundaries within which a researcher shall study the problem with the predetermined objective in view."[20]

---

20. Kothari, *Research Methodology*, 27.

However, defining the problem is not so a simple task! It is a herculean task the researcher has to engage in before commencing the research process. Yet, it is a crucial part of the research if the researcher needs to perform a sound research and needs time, attention, and due weight. An Indian theorist of research C. R. Kothari in his book *Research Methodology* lists some techniques which the researcher can use in an endeavor to define his/her problem for research. I list and describe them below:

First, *the researcher should make a statement of the problem in a general way*. By making a statement in a general way Kothari thinks about the movement of the researcher from the idea in his/her mind towards a wider and general statement of the problem. At this point, the researcher immerses oneself into the whole problem in its wider sense. In the case of field research work, the researcher may perform a pilot search of the situation in order to understand the broadness of the problem, which in turn will help him/her in his/her endeavor to narrow down the problem. Therefore, the process of narrowing the problem discussed in the previous subsection is a process of defining the problem.

Second, *the researcher should endeavor to understand the nature and origin of the problem*. This is another step in the researcher's task of defining the research problem. In this step, the researcher struggles to understand the problem, its origin and its nature. According to Kothari, "The best way of understanding the problem is to discuss it with those who first raised it in order to find out how the problem originally came out and with what objectives in view."[21] Therefore, through visiting the locations where the problem is experienced before executing the research proper and having some discussions with the interlocutors of the problem will enable the researcher understand both the nature and the origin of the research problem.

Third, *the researcher should survey the available literature*. Before the researcher defines the problem he/she needs to have a general survey of existing literature relating to the intended research problem. I can call this survey as 'primary literature review' with the intention of gaining a wider knowledge about the problem. This primary literature search is important in at least two ways: One, the researcher will gain knowledge from other researchers who have struggled with similar problems in his/her area of study. Two, it will help the researcher know the reports, theories, and explanations of other researchers in such a way that he/she will not recapitulate what others have done. Therefore, the existing researches may be good indicators of the types

21. Ibid.

of problems which the researcher should expect or the promises which are possible in his/her newly initiated research in furthering knowledge.

Since no academic research can be built on the vacuum, the research problem needs to have a relation with the current research trends or theory. The literature survey will make the researcher orient oneself in current issues relating to the selected problem. This search for connection with the existing literature or theory will enable the researcher to provide a thorough description of the problem in line with the existing knowledge or theories about the problem.

Fourth, the researcher should develop the research idea through discussions with others. The researcher is not the only person to define the problem. If the researcher subjects the problem to a discussion with other researchers in his/her field of study, it is possible that new ideas can emerge. These ideas can help the researcher to refine his/her research problem towards a clearer and more understandable one. Kothari calls this discussion with other colleagues 'experience survey' whereby the researcher gains more knowledge and clarity about the problem through the experiences and knowledge of other researchers. In this case, the discussion partners help the researcher to focus his/her thinking about the problem into specific aspects with his/her field of study.

Fifth, *the researcher should re-phrase the research problem.* After having gained insights from the previous steps, the researcher needs now to sit down and rephrase his/her research problem into a more clear and well-understandable proposition. Kothari encourages us that "Once the nature of the problem has been clearly understood, the environment (which the problem has got to be studied) has been defined, discussions over the problem have taken place and the available literature has been surveyed and examined, rephrasing the problem into analytical or operational terms is not a difficult task."[22]

In summary, Kothari puts forth five other important points to take into account while the researcher endeavors to define the research problem. These points are the following:

a. Technical terms and words or phrases, with special meanings used in the statement of the problem, should be clearly defined.

b. Basic assumptions or postulates (if any) relating to the research problem should be clearly stated.

22. Ibid, 28.

    c.   A straight forward statement of the value of the investigation (i.e. the criteria for the selection of the problem) should be provided.

    d.   The suitability of the time-period and the sources of data available must also be considered by the researcher in defining the problem.

    e.   The scope of the investigation or the limits within which the problem is to be studied must be mentioned explicitly in defining the research problem.[23]

Therefore, the above descriptions about defining the problem for research indicate that the problem for research is a very important part in the research process. This means that the research problem needs to be handled with care before the researcher decides to embark in the process of research proper.

Conclusion

The way to select a researchable problem depending on the researcher's available time, and without incurring too much costs has been the sole purpose of this chapter. The chapter has discussed ways through which the researcher can use in order to select a suitable problem. The chapter has also put forth the issue of narrowing the problem from the more general idea to a more specific and researchable question that can be defined easily. Hence, the sole concern of the chapter was to describe ways in which the researcher can formulate a convincing and reliable research problem.

Chapter Highlights

1. The first place to start in order to obtain a reasonable research problem from the real life of the people is conducting a 'reconnaissance.' Reconnaissance is a pre-visit to the research area before the real research is conducted.

2. A research question or problem is anything that is not in the way it is supposed to be. This can be a situation, state of affairs, or a difficulty of some sort that needs to be solved.

3. In order for the researcher to get a specific issue to study, he/she needs to narrow it down the broad selected topic. Narrowing the research problem

23. Ibid, 29.

or topic means focusing the research into its few manageable aspects according to the time limit available.

4. The narrowed problem needs to be defined clearly. Defining the research problem is stating it in the view of its boundaries. It is laying down boundaries within which the researcher shall study the problem.

Study Questions

1. Select one broad research problem and narrow it down as much as possible to suit your ability to carry out research.

2. Why do you think it is important to define the research problem selected?

3. Discuss, in a more detail, the benefits of conducting a reconnaissance.

6

Writing a Literature Review Section

"A literature review is a written document that presents a logically argued case founded on a comprehensive understanding of the current state of knowledge about a topic of study. This case establishes a convincing thesis to answer the study's question."

—MACHI & MCEVOY, *THE LITERATURE REVIEW*, 4.

Introduction

AFTER SELECTING THE RESEARCH topic or question, the researcher needs to review the existing literature. Literature review is important in a field research process. This is an exiting moment to interact with other researchers in the field of study in a more detailed and analytical focus. In this chapter we discuss the ways in which the researcher can use in order to interact with other researchers. We begin by providing the definition of literature review, its functions in the research process, its components and the purpose of having such components. We also discuss the ways in which the researcher can use to write a good and convincing literature review and how to evaluate simple arguments within other people's written reports. We end up this chapter with the ways in which the researcher can organize his/her literature review document. Since literature review is one of the important parts of the research process, this chapter provides the necessary clues on the way the researcher can write effective and convincing literature reviews.

What Is Literature Review?

But, what is literature review in the general sense of research? There are various definitions of literature review depending on the field of study. One outstanding definition in the humanities and in sociological studies is that of Chris Hart. According to Hart, literature review is the "selection of available documents (both published and unpublished) on the topic, which contain information, ideas, data, and evidence written from a particular standpoint to fulfil certain aims or express certain views on the nature of the topic and how it is to be investigated, and the effective evaluation of these documents in relation to the research being proposed."[1]

Another more resent definition is that of Laurence A. Machi and Brenda T. McEvoy. Machi and McEvoy define literature review thus: "*A literature review is a written document that presents a logically argued case founded on a comprehensive understanding of the current state of knowledge about a topic of study. This case establishes a convincing thesis to answer the study's question.*"[2]

In research, literature review is not an argument that provides the new knowledge that the researcher expects in his/her research. Even though the reviewer will briefly explain the primary purpose of his/her research in the literature review, this purpose is not expected to point to the possible outcomes of the research.

Following the above definitions of literature review, we can state that even though literature review may summarize some ideas from literature read, it is not primarily a descriptive list of papers just providing summaries of such papers. It is not just a list of literature and an endeavor to describe each of them in detail. In general sense, literature review is not an annotated bibliography of literature one has studied. Rather, it is a critical "looking again" (re-viewing) at what other researchers have done. Its organization is mainly based on *ideas* brought by those various literatures flowing from particular period of time to another. In this case, literature review should indicate the 'genre of knowledge', i.e. the flow of discoveries of knowledge about a particular phenomenon in a particular field of study at a particular time span. Literature review should indicate that the researcher is aware how his/her research work is linked/not linked with existing published literature.

---

1. Hart, *Doing Literature Review*, 13.
2. Machi & McEvoy, *The Literature Review*, 4 (italics is in original).

Functions of Literature Review

What exactly is the function of literature review in research? Despite linking research with other published researches, literature review has other functions. We will discuss these functions as outlined by Meredith D. Gall, Walter R. Borg and Joyce P. Gall:[3] First, It should help to narrow the Research Problem: Always researchers tend to construct broad research problems as their starting points. If such topics are left without narrowing and are used in the research, as stated earlier, they can lead to superficial results. Literature review broadens the scope of the researcher and makes him/her focus in a specific point of view. This is because the researcher will learn from reviews of other researchers and how they constructed fruitful lines of inquiry in their own broad fields of interest. In this case, the literature review makes the researcher able to adopt a single narrowed point of view stipulated in a certain problem of his/her interest.

Second, literature review should help the researcher to acquire his/her own line of inquiry. We stated earlier that researchers begin with broad problems, problems with a number of lines of inquiry. Through surveying the works of other researchers, some of the lines of inquiry already taken by others will be identified. This will help the researcher to construct his/her own line of inquiry that makes a contribution to the existing lines of inquiries. It will be possible for the researcher to construct a new and different line of inquiry because of his/her experience, which can, in most cases, be different from that of other existing researchers. Moreover, none of the existing researches is expected to be exhaustive. In this case, the perspectives or lines of inquiry overlooked by other researchers will possibly be identified and followed by the researcher.

Third, literature review should help the researcher get ride of less effective approaches. Through literature review the researcher will come into contact with several approaches to his/her problem attempted by other researchers. Some of these approaches will have been used repeatedly in a course of years. The researcher will avoid recapitulating similar approaches that probably proved less useful in their time of use, or that can hardly work more efficiently in the researcher's time and context.

Fourth, literature review helps the researcher in designing his/her own methodological perspective. A methodological perspective is not a particular method or a technique that the researcher uses in investigating

3. Gall, Borg & Gall, *Educational Research*, 114–116.

a particular problem. But, it is a philosophy of the study in general. It is a general approach through which the researcher uses to investigate a particular problem.[4] Literature review will widen the researcher into different philosophies or methodologies of the existing researches. In having this wide spectrum, the researcher will have a wide chance to construct his/her methodological perspective.

Fifth, literature review should help the researcher to identify and build his/her research on the recommendations of the existing researches. Almost all research reports conclude by re-discussing the main issues rose in the study, identifying the main problems and strengths of the research process, especially in trying to deal with the research problem. Eventually, the conclusions provide some recommendations for further research on the problem or on some of the issues raised by the research. These recommendations are important for the researcher when reviewing the literature. The researcher can build his/her research on the existing recommendations, but constructing his/her own perspective on those recommendations.

Sixth, literature review should help the researcher gain support on the grounded theory constructed or expected to be constructed. Many researches are designed in a way that they test a theory or construct a new theory from data gained from the research. A theory constructed from data obtained during research is called Grounded Theory.[5] In order to support the theory constructed, the literature review is not done beforehand. It is done when data has been collected and analyzed for interpretation and reporting. It is in the process of reporting that some other literatures are reviewed to see what they say about the obtained data. In this case, the data obtained and the theory constructed are contextualized in the points of views present in the existing literature. In regard to this thinking, one of the founders of the grounded theory, Barney G. Glaser says thus concerning the way literature review is done: "[W]e collect the data in the field first. Then we start analyzing it and generating theory. When the theory seems sufficiently grounded and developed, *then* we review the literature in the field and relate theory to it through the integration of ideas. . . . Thus scholarship in the same area starts after the emerging theory is sufficiently developed so the theory will not be preconceived by pre-empting concepts."[6] According to Glaser, the literature review done after the research has been conducted

---

4. Gobo, *Doing Ethnography*, 18.
5. Glaser and Strauss, *The Discovery of Grounded Theory* (1967).
6. Glaser in Gall, Borg & Gall, *Educational Research*, 116.

and the data analyzed means to support the theory constructed or refine it in order to contribute to the existing knowledge or theories.

Components of Effective Literature Review

Having discussed the way literature review is helpful to the researcher, it is important to discuss the components of a convincing literature review. What makes a convincing literature review? The convincing literature review is relative; it mainly depends on the reader and his/her interests and specialties. In most cases, the convincing literature review should accomplish the following aspects:

First, it should be *critical* and *evaluative* of what has been published in relation to the topic of research which the researcher has currently chosen to deal with.

Second, its main purpose should be to *summarize, synthesize* and *analyze* the arguments of other authors who have written about the topic before the researcher can embark in his/her own argument.

Third, it should *describe* and *analyze* the existing knowledge about the phenomenon under study and *point out the existing gap* (i.e. what is not yet done) in research, that urgently needs to be done, and that will possibly be accomplished by the researcher (in contributing to the existing knowledge about the phenomenon).

Fourth, through reading and rereading of published literature, the review should *uncover* the *similarities* and *differences, consistencies* and *inconsistencies,* or *controversies* emerging in the previously done research. Therefore, the literature review is expected to assess previous studies about the phenomenon and critically discuss strengths and weaknesses of such studies.

Purpose of Writing a Literature Review Section

What is the purpose of doing a literature review in the research process? The above-listed components of a convincing literature review suggest for the purpose of a literature review in doing research on a particular topic. Chris Hart states thus about the reason for reviewing literature in the research process: "One of the main reasons for writing the literature review is to make a proposal for the research you intend to do. This means that your review of the literature must provide a methodological rationalization for your research. You need, then, to demonstrate that you understand the history of your topic.

It is your responsibility to investigate this history in order to provide the story of how the topic was defined, established and developed."[7]

Machi and McEvoy, adding to the above statement, have this to say about the purpose of literature review: "The basic literature review (. . .) summarizes and evaluates the existing knowledge on a particular topic. Its purpose is to produce a position on the state of that knowledge; this is the thesis."[8] In this case, literature review provides the scholarship context of the question to be studied and demonstrates that the researcher is aware of the existing researches in his/her field of study. It helps readers to understand that the topic in question has been of interest among researchers.

This is also what Meredith D. Gall, Walter R. Borg and Joyce P. Gall suggest in their book *Educational Research: An Introduction*. These researchers have this to say: "Unless your study builds on the work of other researchers in your area of inquiry, it is very unlikely to contribute to research knowledge."[9] Quoting Joel Levin and Hermione Marshall, Gall, Borg and Gall emphasized their point thus: "For research to make a substantial contribution, it must be based on adequate knowledge of the field, and the study's introduction must reflect this knowledge . . . Unfortunately, we sometimes receive manuscripts from investigators who base their research on early work that is now dated or from researchers who ignore current work. Reviewers may then be left questioning why the study was conducted, which usually leads to a recommendation of rejection."[10]

A Convincing Literature Review

Gall, Borg, and Gall's statements above stand as precautions for researchers to allocate enough time in preparing both substantial and convincing literature review. According to them, a convincing literature review should not only be theoretically attractive, but also substantial in the sense that it contributes something significant to the existing knowledge. Hence, a convincing literature strives to fill the gap of knowledge by extensively surveying the existing knowledge and building on such knowledge.

A convincing literature review should strive to explain exhaustively what is covered by the main topic of the planned study. It is quite obvious

7. Hart, *Doing Literature Review*, 173.

8. Machi & McEvoy, *The Literature Review*, 2.

9. Gall, Borg & Gall, *Educational Research*, 114.

10. Levin and Marshall in Gall, Borg & Gall, *Educational Research*, 114.

that no single literature review can ever be written by a human being that covers everything on a particular topic. This is because publications are being produced today and then, new ideas emerge today and then, and scholars change their minds about the world today and then. What is expected in the exhaustive literature review is the way the author strives to cover all the main issues in the topic in regard to the existing scholarship.[11]

Since ideas evolve day and night, it is important that the author of literature review carefully examines his/her sources. The important question to ask oneself is what authorities and sources are relevant to the chosen topic in this area of study? This means that the literature review needs to be based on authoritative voices in the area of study. It has to criticize and evaluate these voices as a way forward towards creating new knowledge about the topic. Moreover, such prominent voices have to be selected in consideration of the existing paradigms and research traditions they represent. This means that the reviewed literature should be prominent voices in the paradigm and tradition into which the researcher is currently working. Therefore, a convincing literature review needs to take into account the integrity of the reviewed sources, the paradigm and traditions which those sources belong and the types of methodologies and theories employed by such sources.[12]

A convincing literature review strives to be fair in the way the author treats authors of the reviewed literature. The author does not need to approach the literature of a certain author with his/her preconceived ideas about that author. These will hinder him/her from reading it subjectively. The reviewer should not be satisfied with only one book or article of the author presuming that he/she knows the whole idea of that author. Since ideas are in the authors' minds, the reviewer needs to read several literatures about one particular author in order to grasp fully the whole main idea of that author. This reading and grasping of the whole main idea of the author will help the reviewer in his/her own reasoning and evaluation of the author's argument.[13]

---

11. Mouton, *How to Succeed*, 90.

12. Pazmiño, *Doing Theological Research*, 11–12. A curious and serious literature reviewer mostly begins with the examination of the footnotes or bibliographical entries of the sources that the researcher wants to review. Footnotes and bibliographical entries will help the researcher to trace the origin of ideas used by the sources. In so doing, the researcher ensures that he/she is working within the right research paradigm and tradition (see Pazmiño, *Doing Theological Research*, 11).

13. Mouton, *How to Succeed*, 90.

A convincing literature review should consult online sources but should not depend entirely on these sources.[14] Despite the internet sources the reviewer should primarily strive to use published standard journals and published prominent books. This means that a literature review should draw ideas about the topic from a variety of authors, and from a variety of types of literature.[15]

A convincing literature review should present ideas in an organization that the reader can understand. A well organized literature review does not bore the reader. It encourages him/her to continue reading and continue enjoying the presentation of its argument. It should be born in mind that mere listing of books one has read, or mere construction of a summary of those books and presenting that summary is not adequate to make a convincing literature review. A logical presentation, not of the summary or list of books but of the argument of the literature review, is required to make a good literature review.[16] In this case, the literature review in itself needs to be an argument with a definite structure that convinces the reader about the knowledge and critical stance of the reviewer.

Hart observes that a well-structured argument of the literature review accomplishes two important aspects in research: indicating the reviewer's knowledgeability of the past definitions and assumptions, and the identifying argumentational aspects of what is known. Hart list the components of the two aspects indicated by a structured argument of a literature review thus:

Knowledge-based elements:

1. a description of previous work on the topic, identifying leading concepts, definitions and theories;

2. consideration of the ways in which definitions were developed and operationized as solutions to the problems seen in the previous work;

3. identification and description of matters other researchers have considered important.

Argumentation elements:

1. a description of what you find wrong in previous work on the topic;

---

14. Machi & McEvoy, *The Literature Review*, 42–43.

15. Mouton, *How to Succeed*, 91.

16. Ibid.

2. a proposal for action that might solve the problem—your research;

3. an explanation of the benefits that might result from adopting the proposal;

4. a refutation of possible objections to the proposal.[17]

However, in the process of identifying the 'gap in knowledge' about a particular phenomenon and constructing a literature review argument, one has to analyze and evaluate other researcher's arguments. The "gap in knowledge is the inadequacy of existing scientific theories and laws to describe, explain, or predict a social phenomenon under investigation."[18] This can be found through analyzing other researchers' literatures. Analyzing other researchers' arguments requires careful reading with a critical eye. Hart drawing from Alec Fisher lists seven methods of reading other researchers' literature in an analytical way. I will list them below as Hart has just presented them:[19]

1. First look quickly through the text in order to get an initial sense of the author's project and purpose.

2. Read the text again circling (. . .) any inference indicators (thus, therefore, etc.) as you read.

3. Look for conclusions and any stated reasons for these. Underline the conclusion and place in brackets < > any reasons.

4. Attempt at this stage to summarize the author's argument. If there is no clear argument, ask what point(s) the author is trying to make and why.

5. Identify what you take to be the conclusions by marking them with a C –remember that there may be interim conclusions as well as the main one. Typical indications of a conclusion are the use of the following words: therefore, thus, hence, consequently, and so on. (. . .).

6. Taking the main conclusion, ask yourself what reasons are presented in the text for believing this conclusion or why you are being asked to accept this conclusion. Typical indications of reasons are words and phrases such as, because, since, it follows, and so on.

17. Hart, *Doing Literature Review*, 174.

18. Ndunguru, *Lectures on Research*, 27.

19. Hart, *Doing Literature Review*, 94.

7. The reasons provided for the argument can be ranked into a structure. Go through each reason (R) asking whether it is essential or secondary backing for the argument. From this, you will be left with the core reasons for the argument. You will then be able to construct an argument diagram with the following structure:

   $R_1 + R_2$ = (therefore) C_1 (interim conclusion)

   $C_1 + R_3$ = (therefore) C_2 (main conclusion)"

In his opinion, Mouton adds to the above-mentioned methods that the reviewer should start with a more resent literature going backwards. According to him, starting with a more resent literature enables the reviewer to glance the more resent ideas about the topic and the way such resent ideas built on earlier ones. Mouton maintains that the reviewer should move to reading the abstract, summary or conclusion of the literature in order to get an earlier picture of what the author tries to present. Some headings and references of that literature may also be useful in providing the reviewer the main picture of the literature and why that literature should be taken serious. In order to make sure that the reviewer has understood the book or article or chapter, he/she must be able to reconstruct what he/she has read in his/her own words, especially the main argument of the literature that the reviewer has read.[20]

Doing a Good Literature Review

Machi and McEvoy propose that in order to make a good argument of a literature review the researcher has *to build a case* for the literature review to be produced. What does it mean building a case? Building a case, according to Machi and McEvoy, is "compiling and arranging sets of facts in a logical fashion that will prove the thesis you have made about the research topic."[21]

However, a thesis is a conclusion about facts presented. This conclusion is supported by facts or evidences that lead to building an argument. In this case, "An argument is the logical presentation of evidence that leads to and

20. Mouton, *How to Succeed*, 90.
21. Machi & McEvoy, *The Literature Review*, 60.

justifies a conclusion."[22] Machi and McEvoy propose two types of arguments in a literature review: an argument of discovery, and argument of advocacy.[23]

The argument of discovery, according to Machi and McEvoy deals with issues that already exist, issues already known regarding the topic proposed by the researcher. What the researcher does in presenting this type of argument is to collect the current data known about the topic chosen. If for example the researcher is interested in current effects of stigmatization process in a particular location, the first thing to do is to collect data on what is known regarding the process of stigmatization currently going on in that particular location. In order to make an argument of discovery, the collected data should argue about what is currently known about stigmatization in that particular location.[24]

The argument of Advocacy is built on the argument of Discovery. The argument of Discovery serves the foundational role for which the argument of advocacy is built. This second argument, the argument of advocacy, plays a critiquing role. It critiques the synthesized data in the first argument. The critique done points towards the new direction towards which the research question directs; the critique purports to answer the research question, hence yielding a *thesis statement* of the new research proposed by the researcher.

It is possible for us to use the stigmatization process to explain how the two arguments build up a literature review. The argument of discovery documents what is known about stigmatization in that particular location. It should document as many cases known about stigmatization as possible. The second argument uses these documented data from the first argument to determine which among those cases directs the researcher towards the current effects of stigmatization in that particular location. The conclusion from these two arguments produces a statement that is the basis of your research to be carried.

It should be clear that a scholarly argument is not meant to overpower. It is meant to convince people to believe that what is concluded is sound and logical. Therefore, a scholarly argument should be differentiated from the normal dispute where two people or more are engaged in words in order to try to overpower the other opposing side.

Since the scholarly argument does not aim at overpowering but convincing, it follows a particular pattern that enables it to play a convincing

22. Ibid., 61.
23. Ibid.
24. Ibid.

role. Machi and McEvoy assert that "The persuasive argument is logical. It presents a set of claims backed by sound reasons to support a conclusion. The reasons provided build on solid evidence."[25] Machi and McEvoy argue that arguments are built upon specific rules to determine for their soundness or unsoundness. They state: "The rules of the persuasive argument are simple: if valid reasons are presented that justify the conclusion, the argument is valid. If the reasons are not convincing or if the logic applied fails to support the conclusion, the conclusion is unsound."[26]

After undergoing all the above listed stages, the researcher will have completed the whole analysis. That means trying to know how the author has arranged his/her arguments in terms of providing reasons and conclusions regarding a particular proposition. At this stage there is no question regarding the goodness of the reasons for a particular conclusion because it is not an evaluation stage. The analysis state lays out the structure of an argument.[27] The question still remains: how can the reviewer know when to stop reading the literature for his/her review, or when has the reviewer can claim to have reached the 'saturation' point? Mouton mentions three criteria:

1. When the reviewer has "a repetition of references and authors."

2. When the reviewer finds "no new themes or viewpoints emerge."

3. When the reviewer finds that "secondary reviews, commentators or book reviews confirm what [he/she has] found so far."[28]

Evaluating Simple Arguments

After completing his reading the reviewer needs to evaluate the arguments presented by the authors. Evaluating an argument means questioning the components of the argument (i.e. premises and conclusions) with the question: "what argument (what *you* would need to believe) or evidence (what *you* would need to know) would justify the conclusion?"[29] This question needs to know whether the reasons provided justify the conclusion

---

25. Ibid., 62.

26. Ibid.

27. Hart, *Doing Literature Review*, 94–95.

28. Mouton, *How to Succeed*, 91.

29. Hart, *Doing Literature Review*, 95.

provided. What the reader takes into account in the evaluation of arguments is "whether the conclusion follows from the premises."[30]

Simple arguments have three main parts: *the claim (or Conclusion), the Reasons supported by evidence,* and *the warrant.* Claims provide a declaration about a certain proposed truth about an issue or phenomenon under research.[31] Reasons are statements to explain why the researcher reached the conclusion. Reasons are supported by strong and reliable evidence. Evidence is the data that the researcher obtained in his/her research. The data are assembled in a manner that they provide explanations to support the claim stated. The evidence says that the reasons put forth to support the claim are true. The warrant employs a certain logical line that convinces the reader to accept the claim put forth. It is the 'because' statement. The warrant answers *why* this claim.

How then is the argument evaluated? Machi and McEvoy provide three important questions in evaluating the basic parts of an argument: The first question looks at or identifies the conclusion or claim of the argument. What is the stated conclusion? In identifying the claim, we search for the statement which the author tries to defend in his/her argument. We also search for the qualifiers of that claim. In searching for the qualifiers we look at the argument to see it if it has some words that indicate that the argument recognizes its limits. In such analysis, we ask: Is the claim absolute, or does it have some words or phrases that indicate its limitations in certain circumstances? In trying to find the answer for the above question, we will easily identify between careful and less careful arguers. Less careful arguers can easily resort to absolute claims while careful arguers are sensitive to limitations of their claims.

Example: Most librarians are good people.

The above statement is a claim. It claims that librarians are good people. However, it is aware that not all librarians are good people. The word 'most' indicates the limitation to that claim. It shows that the claim is limited to some librarians not all.

The second question looks at the reasons that support the reached conclusion or claim of the argument. What are those reasons that the researcher puts forth in order to support his/her conclusion? Here the analyst

30. Ibid.

31. For more description about the types of claims, see Machi & McEvoy, *The Literature Review*, 66–68.

lists all the reasons provided in order to support the claim, and then examines the strength of these reasons. If the claim was clearly identified, it
will be easy to find the reasons. The reasons follow after the word 'because.'
What is before this word is the claim of the argument? The analyst asks
oneself: why does the author put forth this claim? Any statement that tries
to answer this question is the reason provided. In the case of the previous
claim, for example, we can list several reasons:
Most librarians are good people because:

- they have a welcoming language to library users.

- they have attended courses for librarianship

- they are always with people, etc.

After listing the reasons, the analyst examines the weight of the reasons
provided. Here two questions are important: first, are the reasons provided
good enough to support the claim of the argument provided by the author.
Second, are the reasons provided relevant to the claim? It is possible to
provide very good and well-arranged reasons. However, it is not easy to
provide relevant reasons. The analyst needs to analyze the relevance of the
reasons in regard to the claim of the argument and how good that reason is
in supporting that claim.

The third question looks at or examines the relationship between the
reasons stated and the conclusion reached. It examines whether the reasons
provided for the claim made are convincing to the reader, and the conclusion
reached follows from those reasons. The questions at this stage are: Do the
reasons put forth by the researcher in his/her argument argue for the conclusion reached? Reasons must have data to support them. Do those reasons
in the researcher's argument have enough data to support them? Data are
evidences to say that the reasons stated hold a grain of truth. Having provided the reasons and data to support them, follows the question whether the
conclusion reached follows from the reasons and evidence provided: is the
conclusion derived from the stated reasons and evidence provided?[32]

---

32. Machi & McEvoy, *The Literature Review*, 62–63.

Figure 1: Examples on Evaluating an Argument

Argument 1

Leadership needs patient people for success to be visible. Success in the leadership process will depend on the patience of its leaders. Patient leaders enable things to go smoothly in organizations. When organizations get patient leaders, they succeed in most of their plans.

Evaluation:

The first question requires us to look at the conclusion stated. What is the conclusion? The above statements are all claims for something: patience of leaders and success in organizations. If we ask the second question that requires reasons for the claim, we can note that there are no reasons stated. If we ask the third question that requires the conclusion to be drawn from the reasons, which are in turn supported by evidence or data, we see that there are no evidence that support that there is a relationship between the patience of leaders and success. Therefore, the argument stated above is unsound because it lacks the necessary qualities of a sound argument.

Argument 2

One important reason for the need of patient people in leadership is that to lead is to influence other people towards a certain goal. Another reason for that is that most impatient leaders give up in the process. Therefore, leadership needs patient people for success to be visible.

Evaluation:

The first question is about the conclusion. Is there a conclusion stated in this argument? The last sentence in the argument is the conclusion or claim of the argument. The statement claims that patient leaders are the ones that enable success to be visible during the leadership process. The second question in the evaluation process requires us to look if there are any reasons stated for the claim or conclusion provided. The first and second sentences are the reasons: patient leaders are needed because influence towards success depends very much on patient leaders, and that patient leaders are needed because success needs people that can persevere emerging hardships. However, there are no data to support the stated reasons. Therefore, this argument is also unsound.

Argument 3

One important reason for the need of patient people in leadership is that to lead is to influence other people towards a certain goal. Another reason for that is that most impatient leaders give up in the process. Masenga who carried out research among Non-Governmental organizations in Njombe Region found that 90% of effective organizations had leaders with high integrity and patience. Only 10% were effective without having patient leaders. This indicates that leadership needs patient people for success to be clearly visible.

Evaluation:

The first question is about whether the conclusion has been stated. In the above argument the conclusion is found in the last sentence: leadership needs patient people for success to be clearly visible. The second question asks whether the conclusion follows from the reasons provided. The first and second sentences are the reasons. The conclusion seems to be drawn from the two stated reasons. The conclusion follows from the reasons. Moreover, reasons stated are supported by the data that Masenga obtained in his research among Non-Governmental organizations in Njombe Region regarding the relationship between the patience of leaders in their leadership process and the success of organizations they lead. Hence, this argument is a sound argument.

Having illustrated on the way in which the researcher can go about evaluating an argument basing on the claim and the reasons provided, let us now discuss further about the evidence that supports the reasons for the claim. Evidence needs to be strong and supportive. It should not just be based on only personal beliefs, or personal opinions about an issue or phenomenon. Evidence is not merely the data (pieces of information) that the researcher obtained, but the arrangement of that data to support the reasons for a claim stated. Evidence is the data collected for a special purpose or agenda.

When the researcher goes to the field, he/she collects pieces of information about the research question. His/her aim is mainly to answer that question. Basing on the reasons he/she has, the researcher provides the claim to try answer that question. The most important part of the research process is arranging the obtained data or pieces of information so that they support convincingly that the reasons stated for the claim have a grain of truth. This process of arranging data to support the reasons for the claim is converting data (mere pieces of information that are randomly arranged) into evidence (logically arranged information). Therefore, in order for the researcher to have strong evidence he/she must search for relevant data

(data related to the problem under study) and arrange those data in a logic that supports the reasons for providing the claim or a particular viewpoint.

In order for the data to provide a strong and convincing evidence for the reasons about a claim, their quality should be high. When we talk of the quality of the data, we mainly refer to their credibility regarding the case we are trying to make. Machi and McEvoy provide three points to elaborate the characteristics of high-quality data: accuracy, preciseness, and authority. In their own words they state: "High-quality data are accurate. They present a true picture of the phenomenon being studied and are unbiased report of an objective observation. High-quality data are precise. They provide an exact measurement, description, or depiction of the phenomenon. High-quality data are authoritative. They are a product of sound research practice."[33] Basing on the three characteristics of high-quality data stated by Machi and McEvoy above, one can also determine the quality of the argument provided by the researcher because the quality of the argument depends sorely on the quality of data that support the reasons for the claim or conclusion.

Therefore, after analyzing the claim and the reasons, the analyst will have to analyze the evidence basing on the above criteria of high quality data. In analyzing the evidence, the analyst lists the evidence itself and examines the strength of that evidence. Here the analyst asks oneself: what is the evidence provided for the reasons? The evidence should include: data, examples, cases, citations from authorities, speeches, the results from interviews, questionnaires, and observations, one's personal lived experiences, constitutions, statutes, and court rulings, organization's policies, etc. In a more general sense, evidence is whatever provided by the author in order to make readers believe in the reasons for the claim. These kinds of information need to be provided after each reason in order to support it. Therefore the analyst looks at these information and lists them.

In the process of examining the evidence, the analyst further examines the goodness of that evidence: is the evidence good, or sufficient to carry the weight of the reasons? Are they enough for this or these reasons? Then, is the evidence relevant to the reasons provided? It does not matter how many paragraphs the author has written, what matters is the sufficiency and the relevance of the evidence to the stated reasons.

33. Ibid., 71 cf. Rubin & Rubin, *Qualitative Interviewing*, 261.

Organizing Your Literature Review Section

After discussing the literature review as a document that should present an informed argument putting more emphasis on the way in which the reviewer can evaluate the authors' arguments, it is also important to consider the ways in which the reviewer can present that argument in order to convince his/her readers. Several ways may be used in structuring the presentation of the results of his literature readings. Mouton mentions several ways, five of these ways are the following:[34]

Organizing by Chronology.

Chronology has to do with age, which started and which followed. The reviewer should begin presenting ideas from the oldest literature upwards. This is different from the reading process whereby the reviewer begins with the more resent literature downwards. Organizing by chronology is simple and most preferred way. The researcher just looks at the literature reviewed, which of them is the older followed by which one, and which is the most resent of all of them.

Organizing by Following School of Thought, Theory or Definition of Ideas

Different schools may have different thoughts about an idea. The reviewer may organize his/her review following the way a particular school of thought theorizes or defines that idea. In this organization, the reviewer can trace the origin of that idea and the way it developed among different schools to the present time. Since the reviewer traces the development of ideas among schools of thought, he/she will have the chance at the end of his/her review to present his/her position in relation to the different existing positions.

Organizing Thematically

The reviewer may construct small themes from the main theme and present his/her review following those themes. The themes presented need to

34. Mouton, *How to Succeed*, 92–95.

be arranged in a way that reflects the argument of the review report and should be clear and well-sequenced in such a way that it does not confuse the reader of the review report. The themes drawn should neither be confusing nor contradicting to each other. This means that the themes that the researcher uses to present his/her review should be precise, clear, and to the point. One theme should not hold many ideas in such a way that the reader fails to recognize which ideas to take into account within the one theme. Therefore, organizing thematically calls attention to the researcher to be careful and consistent.

Organizing by Hypothesis

The reviewer may organize his/her review by following the various hypotheses put forth by other reviewers in the search for answers to their own questions. In following this way, the reviewer does not look at the conclusions that other reviewers have reached in relation to those hypotheses. He/she looks at the evidence to support each hypothesis. The reviewer is interested in what evidence supports which hypothesis. However, the arrangement needs to be logical, precise and consistent. The flow of ideas within the literature review section need to be cohesive and fluently arranged. This way of organizing enables the reviewer to construct his/her own hypothesis.

Organizing by Method Used in the Study

Not all studies use the same method. Even those that use the same method still obtain slightly different results. In reviewing the literature, the reviewer can arrange his/her review following the various methods used in various studies about the problem and the results they obtained. The reviewer, through these methods, may have the chance to compare them and suggest his/her own method, and the reasons for selecting such a method. The important thing to remember is that the methods used in constructing the literature review should be arranged in such a way that they portray a good flow of materials in the review. In doing that the organization of the review by method becomes useful and helpful.

Conclusion

The concern of this chapter has been to stimulate the researcher's emulous zeal towards examining the existing knowledge. The examination of existing knowledge becomes possible through the examination of other people's researches. This is what literature review is all about.

This chapter has discussed the pros and cons of approaching other people's written works in order to identify the gap of knowledge which the researcher will endeavor to bridge in his/her own research. The chapter has provided a definition of literature review, its functions, its components, its purpose, and the way the researcher can write a convincing literature review. Eventually, the chapter has provided some clues on the way the researcher can evaluate some arguments presented by other researchers. In this case, the chapter is important for researchers because it provides some spotlights on the way to build on other people's researches in order to bring forth new knowledge.

Chapter Highlights

1. The sole concern of literature review is to make a thorough or partial examination of existing literature. This examination enables the researcher to identify the gap of knowledge that is what has not been done in the existing research.

2. The literature review needs to be convincing. This means that the author should strive to be fair in the way he/she treats authors of reviewed literature, organizing in the simplest way possible for the readers to understand.

3. A good literature review must present an argument of discovery and of advocacy. The argument of discovery deals with issues that already exist or issues already known about the topic. The argument of advocacy critiques the synthesized data in the first argument.

4. There are several ways in which the researcher can organize his/her literature review. Some of these ways are: by chronology, by following school of thought, thematically, by hypothesis and by method used by the authors of reviewed literature.

Study Questions

1. Using as many other literatures as possible discuss the importance of doing literature review in the process of doing research.

2. Discuss the features required for a convincing literature review.

3. A literature review may be convincing but not good; it may also be good but not convincing. Discuss this statement using the descriptions provided in this chapter.

7

Designing Your Academic Field Research

"For any investigation, the selection of an appropriate research design is crucial in enabling you to arrive at valid findings, comparisons and conclusions. A faulty design results in misleading findings (. . .)."
—KUMAR, *RESEARCH METHODOLOGY*, 22.

Introduction

NOW THE RESEARCHER HAS identified the research problem, has reviewed the existing literature, and has identified the gap of knowledge. In other words, the researcher has found out what needs to be contributed to existing knowledge. What follows is to design the way the researcher will carry out research in order to make his/her contribution. In this chapter we discuss the various designs which the researcher can use in his/her qualitative field research. We also introduce postmodernism as a current research paradigm before discussing the designs that can be undertaken within this paradigm. In this case, we will discuss some important issues for the researcher to plan the way to execute the field research process.

What Is Research Design?

The genuine research depends sorely on the way the researcher designs his/her research to be executed. The initial question is: What is research design and why is it important in the research process? The response to this question touches the roots of research itself: is there any research without a design? In fact, no efficient research can be carried out without a proper logic of how it is carried out. If such kind of research exists, then it must be like a house built without a foundation.

Kumar writes thus about research: "Research involves systematic, controlled, valid and rigorous exploration and description of what is not known and establishment of associations and causation that permit the accurate prediction of outcomes under a given set of conditions."[1] He also adds: "It also involves identifying gaps in knowledge, verification of what is already known, and identification of past errors and limitations. The strength of *what* you find largely rests on *how* it was found."[2] With this conception in mind, the function of research design becomes visible: it is a starting point in providing answers to the How question about the What of the research.

The *How* question inquires for a procedure or arrangement of things or issues in the research process. It purports to explore the way one anticipates to deal with his/her research question (the *what* of the research) for the sake of seeking possible solutions. Kumar puts it thus: "The main function of a research design is to explain *how* you will find answers [procedure] to your research questions [the what, or the research problem]. The research design sets out the logic of your inquiry."[3] John W. Creswell (2008) adds to Kumar's definition. For him, research design is "the plan or proposal to conduct research, [this plan or proposal] involves the intersection of philosophy, strategies of inquiry, and specific methods."[4] In this case, the research design is expected to consider the philosophical worldview behind the research to be carried (postpositive, post-colonial, post-structuralist, pragmatic, social construction, naturalism, etc), the strategies to be used in the inquiry (inductive, deductive, or inductive and deductive), and the methods of research (instruments of data collection, instruments for data analysis, the way to interpret data, organization f the report and the validity and reliability of the instruments and data).

The philosophical worldviews are influential in the research even though they are not stated in most researches. Creswell quotes Guba to define a 'worldview'. According to his definition, a 'worldview' is a "basic

1. Kumar, *Research Methodology*, 20.
2. Ibid (emphasis is in original).
3. Ibid.
4. Creswell, *Research Design*, 5.

set of beliefs that guide action."[5] Philosophical worldviews are sometimes called 'Epistemologies' and Ontologies' or Paradigms.[6] Making clear the philosophical stand point which the researcher espouses will explain why he/she decided to select Qualitative, Quantitative or Mixed Method strategies for his/her inquiry. When writing a proposal or the research design chapter or section, it is important to describe briefly about a particular worldview of the researcher's choice. Creswell mentions three important aspects to include in the description:

- "The philosophical worldview proposed [or used] in the study.
- A definition of basic considerations of that worldview
- How the worldview shaped their approach to research."[7]

The logic, plan, or proposal of doing research, which Kumar and Creswell have suggested above, is a framework that enables the researcher to attain valid findings that contribute to knowledge. Selecting a proper research design or framework enables the attainment of strong and valid findings. As Kumar convincingly advices: "For any investigation, the selection of an appropriate research design is crucial in enabling you to arrive at valid findings, comparisons and conclusions. A faulty design results in misleading findings (...)."[8] The important aspects in selecting a research design are three: validity, workability, and manageability.[9] Is the design you have selected valid? Is it workable? Can it be manageable within the time frame available?

There are many research designs in this research world, but not all can be valid to all kinds of researches, situations and time limits. Neither can they all be workable and manageable in all conditions, situations and time limits. Hence, the notion of selecting a research design to adopt for particular research context and tradition is crucial.

Research Design and Research Traditions

It should be born in mind that there are four main traditions in qualitative research. Gubrium and Holstein quoted in Bryman have put forth

5. Ibid., 6.
6. Ibid.
7. Ibid.
8. Kumar, *Research Methodology*, 22.
9. Ibid.

the following traditions:[10] first, *natuaralism*, which explore and longs to "understand social reality in its own terms; 'as it really is'; provides reach descriptions of people and interaction in natural settings."[11] This tradition started in United States of America, especially at the University of Chicago's department of sociology. Basing on the positivist assumptions that social reality is 'out there' waiting for the observer to observe and describe it, the researchers in this tradition value nature in their search for knowledge. The natural settings of events, environment and people need to be studied as they are. Therefore we can say that naturalism is the study of nature and the way it portrays itself to the researcher.

The second tradition is *ethnomethodology* which leads the researcher to "understand how social order is created through talk and interaction; has a naturalistic orientation."[12] This tradition has its roots from the philosophical standpoints of phenomenology. Phenomenological standpoints assert that reality is not 'out there' but is socially constructed by people. People always strive to describe the world around them not as it naturally is, but as they make sense of it. Here the researcher "studies the way that participants construct the social world in which they live—how they "create"—rather than trying to describe the social world objectively. In fact, ethnomethodologists do not necessarily believe that we can find an objective reality; instead, how participants come to create and sustain a sense or 'reality' is the focus of the study."[13] This is in contrast to the "ethnographer who seeks to describe the social world as the participants see it, the ethnomethodologist seeks to maintain some distance from that world."[14]

Ethnomethodology is also different from naturalism. The main difference is based on the focus. "The focus shifts from the scenic features of everyday life onto the ways through which the world comes to be experienced as real, concrete, factual, and 'out there.'"[15] Therefore ethnomethodology studies events not basing on particular scenes and their natural settings on those scenes, but as real, factual and concrete out there. This

10. Bryman, *Social Science Research*, 277.

11. Ibid., 267.

12. Ibid.

13. Chamblis & Schutt, *Making Sense*, 211.

14. Ibid.

15. Ibid.

means that the "ethonomethodologist focuses on how reality is constructed, not on what it is."[16]

The third tradition is *emotionalism*. This tradition "exhibits a concern with subjectivity and gaining access to 'inside' experience; [and] concern with the inner reality of humans."[17] The tradition is mainly concerned with the psychic part of the human being. Its main role is to learn the way humans feel in their inner experiences of particular phenomena. Therefore emotionalism touches the inner experience of the person and how such person can describe it in his/her own words.

The fourth tradition is *postmodernism*. This tradition holds "an emphasis on 'method talk'; [and it is] sensitive to the different ways social reality can be constructed."[18] Postmodernism is an overarching tradition researchers find themselves in the twenty first century. It is the tradition we are in now. Its main emphasis is on the multiplicity and relativity of meaning, methods, and ways of living. It questions the taken for granted phenomena in order to ascertain their alternatives. Instead of viewing explanations or reality as being the only permanent ones, postmodernism views them as alternatives to many such ways. "The social world itself," writes Bryman, "is viewed as a context out of which many accounts can be hewn."[19] Bryman adds: "As a result, 'knowledge' of the social world is relative; any account is just one of many possible ways of rendering social reality."[20] The emphasis on method for studying a problem in social research in the postmodern tradition is because reality cannot be viewed in only one point of view. The researcher needs to specify what point of view does the researcher try to understand the problem and through which methodological stance.

Research Traditions and Research Paradigms

It is of vital importance for researchers to understand in which *paradigm* they are carrying out their research enterprise. This is because each paradigm has its ways of understanding and interpreting the world. Paradigms in research should not be mixed; the researcher has to carry out research following only one paradigm. The above traditions in qualitative field

16. Ibid.

17. Bryman, *Social Science Research*, 267.

18. Ibid.

19. Ibid., 498.

20. Ibid.

research represent the various paradigms in research and generation of scientific knowledge. Therefore it is worthwhile for the researcher to choose one among the above paradigms and follow its features in doing science.

The question is: what is a paradigm? According to Thomas Kuhn the word 'paradigm' denotes a revolution in scientific generation of knowledge. "A paradigm is 'a cluster of beliefs and dictates which for scientists in a particular discipline influence what should be studied, how research should be done, [and] how results should be interpreted.'"[21] As a cluster of beliefs, "A paradigm 'defines for a scientific community the types of questions that may legitimately be asked, the types of explanation that are to be sought, and the types of solutions that are acceptable.'"[22] This cluster of beliefs, however, becomes dominant in a particular period of time and place which make the paradigm to exist. "According to Kuhn, when a paradigm is established and researchers engage in 'normal science,' there is little discussion of rules or definitions because they become internalized by researchers working in that paradigm."[23] When the new paradigm emerges, it challenges the existing one forcing it to change the way it dictates scientific practice. At the same time the existing paradigm also resists to the challenge by trying to maintain the existing way of generating knowledge and interpreting it.

The revolution emerges when the new paradigm supersede the existing paradigm by proving that its ideas are worthwhile and people should take their attention towards them. The revolution forces contemporary researchers to adhere to the existing paradigm in whatever they think and act about science. An example of paradigm change is the movement of scientific thinking from Modern to post-modern paradigms. This shift can be considered as a paradigm change from thinking and acting in the way scientists did in the modern era towards another way of thinking in the post-modern era. However, as I have just said, resistance to this shift is inevitable. Most practitioners of science can remain rigid to change, trying to maintain the modern way of thinking and doing science.

In qualitative field research, the above traditions arose because of the challenges which emerged on the course of thinking and researching. Naturalism for example is a way of thinking embraced by a certain school of thought that begun at the University of Chicago between 1930 and 1940.

21. Ibid., 453 cf. Mannion, *Ecclessiology and Postmodernity*, 5–6 & Pazmiño, *Doing Theological Research*, 11–12.

22. Kee, *Christian Origins*, 176 footnote 26.

23. Ciulla, "Leadership Ethics," 10.

It was their paradigm. Ethnomethodology is a way of thinking of another school of thought which tries to resist naturalistic thinking, and so are emotionalism and postmodernism. The above described traditions should be considered to be the results of dissatisfaction of the practitioners of science on the way science is being practiced in a particular place at a particular time. It is an endeavor at trying to find alternative ways of understanding and expressing the world. Therefore, from this development in challenging the older traditions towards the better one possible, postmodernism is the current paradigm of the way knowledge is generated, interpreted, and shared in various places of the world.

Postmodernism as the Current Research Paradigm

Since postmodernism is the current paradigm into which most researchers adhere, it is better to define it and discuss its features. What is postmodernism and which are its feature? This is a cunning question that leads us to the discussion of the components of this paradigm. The word 'postmodernism' was coined by Frederico de Onis in 1934. His aim was "to describe Spanish and Latin American poetry between 1905 and 1914 which reacted against modernism (. . .)."[24] According to John R. Gibbins and Bo Reimer postmodernism may refer to:

- aesthetic and architectural movements or cultures (. . .); or to a cultural avante garde or elite movement whose cry was 'everything goes' (. . .).

- popular phenomena in which consumer life-styles and mass consumption dominate taste and fashion, and in which groups stress difference and distinction in their attempt to accumulate cultural capital (. . .).

- a general cultural orientation with special recognition of the new self and groups rooted in the economic and political context of late modernity, with significant expressions in political culture as well as life-styles (. . .).

- spirit of the age (. . .), or to an historical period, variously described as starting around 1875 (. . .) and prevailing until some unspecified future time (. . .).[25]

24. Gibbins & Reimer, *The Impact of Values*, 306.
25. Ibid.

All the above aspects are significant attempts to understand what it means by postmodernism. However, Gibbins and Reimer summarize the above aspects in one understanding of postmodernism "as a general cultural orientation, which emerges from the wider contextual arguments provided by interpreting postmodernism as referring to the phenomena of mass popular culture and the spirit of the age. (. . .) the expression of postmodernism in aesthetic or architectural movements, or among the avante garde, [are regarded] as exemplars."[26] According to Gerard Mannion, "The postmodern era is thus marked by a shift from belief in certainties and truth claims to more localised and piecemeal factors. The individual is seen as creating his or [her] own meaning to a certain extent, rather than receiving it from without."[27]

Postmodernism has many features which distinguish it from modernity. Some of its features are the following: first, insignificance of distances—people can travel, migrate, and tour anywhere and any time. Technology has made all these possible. Second, the homogenization of cultural values which leads to the emergence of one super culture. The mass media such as televisions, videos, film, and music are the main instruments for the construction of the postmodern self. Third, the compression of time-space—the world is shrinking to become a global village. Activities that were localized only in cities are now also available in local communities. The fourth feature is the emphasis on relativity, and the existence of alternative values for every aspect. Nothing is permanent. The world and its components is in the process of change leading to new culture, new technology, new political orientations, new ways of communicating and even new understanding of the same world. The fifth feature doubts to anything which is taken for granted.

Generally, postmodernists claim that the political, social, cultural, technological and economic world is always in a state of change. Among the many assumptions of postmodernism include "anti-essentialism, anti-foundationalism, and anti-rationalism, and changes hinging upon re-evaluating the role of language and discourse in the creation of meaning, the self, behaviour, and order (. . .)."[28] There is an emphasis on subject matters that were previously ignored, such as: "The deviant, the odd or quirky, the forgotten

26. Ibid.

27. Mannion, *Ecclessiology and Postmodernity*, 4.

28. Gibbins & Reimer, *The Impact of Values*, 305.

or suppressed, or the relatively ignored—now attract attention in their own right as well as for the capacity to throw light on the normal (. . .)."[29]

Moreover, there has been a shift in attention. "Attention is given to the everyday; to popular than to élite culture; to alternative rather than to dominant ideologies; to divergent lifestyles rather than to the dominant social order; and to the emerging power of the mass media in constructing and maintaining them (. . .)."[30] Hence, changes emerging are spontaneous and conventional approaches in the mentioned aspects cannot account for these ever-happening changes.

Categories of Field Research Design in the Post-Modern Paradigm

The above description of postmodernism as a paradigm in which we carry out research should guide the researcher in his selection of research design categories and the way he/she should design his research. Kumar identifies some mostly used categories of research designs in our current researches: those which depend on the number of contacts which the researcher has with the study population and those which depend on the reference period which the researcher examines a phenomenon.[31] For the purpose of qualitative field research, we will briefly describe some research design categories falling under the number of contacts which the researcher has with his/her research participants.

The Cross-Section Category

The first is the cross-section category. This is the most commonly used and simple design category in the social sciences and the humanities and whose collected data is easy to process. The main use of the design is on investigating the resurgence or prevalence of a particular social phenomenon, issue, situation or a particular attitude of people in that society. A cross-section design is a suitable design for studying the general picture of the phenomenon studied as it appears during the time when the study is being conducted. Phenomena or issues are studied by taking their cross-section.

29. Ibid.
30. Ibid.
31. Kumar, *Research Methodology*, 93–98.

Why this study design category is called 'cross-section'? It is called so for two reasons: study population considered for study, and time of doing the study. In using a cross-section design category with a particular population:

- Just determine *what* you want to study at that particular time.
- Identify which population or group of people do you want to study.
- Since you cannot study the whole group, select a sample to conduct your study.
- Then, contact the people in the sample in order to inquire for information. You need to have formulated the instrument for data collection before you contact them.

In case of time, a cross-section study involves only a single moment of meeting with the researcher's informants. This means that a cross-section design category enables the researcher to carry out research within a particular time, and is not repeated to the same population and sample. As Kumar notes, the most serious with this category is its inability to ascertain (measure) change. A population examined is not stagnant. The phenomenon examined can change for the better or worse. Cross-section category measures the phenomenon only as it stands during the time the researcher conducts his/her research.

Repeated Contacts or Double Cross-Section Category

The second category is the repeated contacts or double cross-section category. This design category is sometimes called 'the before-and-after' or 'pre-test/post-test' research design category. In this design category, data collection is not done only once within a particular time span; rather, it is repeated more than once within different time spans, mostly two times. Since the study is conducted after having done the first one, it is very suitable for measuring or determining changes in the phenomenon studied within the lapse of time. In this case, the design can enable the researcher to measure or determine the *impact* or *effect* that the phenomenon has had from the first moment he/she did the research to the moment he/she repeats the research within the same population and sample.

It should be born in mind that in the repeated contacts design category the procedures of conducting the study are similar to a cross-section design research. What differentiates the two is the 'number of contacts' the researcher has with informants. While in the cross-section research design the researcher has only one contact, in the repeated contacts design the same researcher has two contacts. This is what makes the repeated research design a 'double cross-section' study.

Despite its advantage as a design category for research (measuring change in the phenomenon and its impact in a particular population at a particular time), the following are some of its disadvantages: first, it is expensive because it involves two encounters with the population or sample. Second, its collected data are more difficult to handle because the researcher will have a large amount of data collected at two distinct moments. Third, the population of study is subject to change within the lapse of time. This can hinder the researcher from obtaining reliable data for measuring the impact of a phenomenon. The point here is that this design category can work well if the population or sample examined remains the same in both phases of data collection.

Longitudinal or Multiple Cross-Section Category

Sometimes the researcher may need to measure the 'trend' or 'pattern' in which a particular phenomenon changes within a particular life of a population and obtaining more accurate and factual information about that population. A repeated research design category cannot enable the researcher to do this because it measures the impact that the phenomenon has only in a particular lapse of time. It does not consider other times in the life of the population. In order to determine the pattern or trend of change that the phenomenon undergoes in a particular population or sample, the researcher has to have several contacts with the study population in a regular interval of time. The number of studies (contacts) with the study population will depend on the researcher's preference.

This design category can be called 'multiple cross-sectional' research design, i.e., it has a process similar to that of cross-section design category in all contacts the researcher makes to his/her research population. The data collected by this design category, however, are not necessarily from the same respondents (sample). They may come from different samples within the same population that the researcher investigates the trend or pattern of the phenomenon within particular respondents he/she will have to carry out multiple cross-sectional studies to those respondents. In this case, the researcher spends much time in the field in his/her endeavor to understand the activities done by his/her research participants.

Qualitative Field Research Designs

Proper designing of a field research depends mainly on the type of qualitative field research undertaken by the researcher. There are several designs of qualitative field researches known, and any design can use any of the above discussed categories in conducting its research. The researcher decides to use a category and a design depending on the context of research and the type of data which the researcher needs in order to answer his/her research questions. This means that not all categories and designs are suitable for all contexts of research. We discuss some of these research designs used in qualitative field research below.

Narrative Research Design

The first design in qualitative field research is narrative research design. This is a design whereby the researcher decides to write an account of a single person or two or three people. The research itself is designed in a way that it provides the account to what the participant(s) has accounted. In this case, the research intended is biographical.

Some of the aspects of this design are the following: first, its main intent is "to discover and understand a phenomenon, process, or the perspectives and worldviews of the people involved" as described by a person two, or three people.[32] Second, the analysis produced does not produce a theory, but identifies recurring themes categories or variables that appear in the data (patterns) for the sake of understanding the phenomenon described. Third, the findings appearing are a mixture of the researchers' (or participants') descriptions and the researchers' analysis of those descriptions. In most cases, the analysis utilizes the "concepts from the theoretical framework of the study."[33] Creswell outlines the underlying principles in any biographical design as follows:

- The lived experiences of interacting individuals are the proper subject matter of sociology.

32. Merriam, *Qualitative Research*, 11.
33. Ibid.

- The meanings of these experiences are best given by the persons who experience them. [The main concern is for] 'meaning and interpretation.'

- Students of the biographical method must learn how to use the strategies and techniques of literary interpretation and criticism . . .

- When an individual writes a biography, he/she writes himself/herself into the life of the subject about whom the individual is writing; the reader reads through her or his perspective.[34]

Creswell also mentions the criteria for assessing a biographical design. These criteria are the following:

- Focus on a single individual (or two or three individuals)

- Collects stories about a significant issue related to this individual's life.

- Develops a chronology that connects different phases or aspects of a story.

- Tells a story that restories a story of the participant in the study.

- Tells a persuasive story told in a literary way.

- Possibly reports themes that build from the story to tell a broader analysis.

- Reflexively brings himself or herself into the study.[35]

Therefore, a well designed biographical research, in most cases, needs to meet the criteria described above.

Ethnographical Research Design

The second qualitative field research design is ethnography. The word 'ethnography' means 'portrait of people.' The word denotes a descriptive study of people and their cultures. Ethnographic research design entails extensive work in the field. In this work the researcher uses formal and informal data collection techniques, that is formal and informal interviewing and observations. The analysis of the data collected takes the perspective of people researched (emic perspective). This design has its underlying assumptions and philosophical backgrounds. I discuss these issues below.

34. Cresswell, *Qualitative Inquiry*, 214.

35. Ibid., 214–15.

Its Philosophical Foundation and Emphasis

Ethnography is built upon the foundation of the philosophy called 'naturalism'. Naturalism is the ethnographers' responses to positivist researchers that used quantitative method as the sole method for verifying and testing theories. Positivists challenged qualitative research of being "inappropriate to social *science*, on the ground that the data and findings it produces are 'subjective', mere idiosyncratic impressions of one or two cases that cannot provide a solid foundation for rigorous scientific analysis."[36]

The emphasis of naturalism is to study reality as it appears in the field without being disturbed by the researcher. According to naturalism as a philosophy, "as far as possible, the social world should be studied in its 'natural' state, undisturbed by the researcher. (. . .). The research must be carried out in ways that are sensitive to the nature of the setting."[37] According to naturalistic view, the "primary aim should be to describe what happens in the setting, how the people involved see their own actions and those of others, and the context in which the actions take place."[38]

Therefore, the intent of ethnography, as a naturalistic study is to study human culture and society, i.e., to study "the beliefs, values and attitudes that structure the behaviour patterns of a specific group of people."[39] The key element of this type of study "is the demand that the social researcher should adopt an attitude of 'respect' or 'appreciation' towards the social world."[40]

Its Meaning in Anthropological Studies

Ethnographic type of research is mostly used by anthropologists who long to present an in-depth social cultural analysis of a particular cultural unit they have selected to study. For anthropologists 'culture' is important because it shapes the lives and behaviors of people in a particular context. In this case, anthropologists study phenomena as they are cultural oriented and cultural significant. Merriam, quoting D'Andrade provides a description of the aspects that identify a phenomenon as being cultural oriented:

36. Hammersley & Atkinson, *Ethnography*, 6.
37. Ibid.
38. Ibid.
39. Merriam, *Qualitative Research*, 13 .
40. Hammersley & Atkinson, *Ethnography*, 6.

To say something is cultural is—at a minimum—to say that it is *shared* by a significant number of members of a social group; shared in the sense of being behaviourally enacted, physically possessed, or internally thought. Further, this something must be recognized in some special way and at least some others are expected to know about it; that is, it must be intersubjectively shared. Finally, for something to be cultural it must have the potential of being passed on to new group members, to exist with some permanency through time and across space.[41]

For anthropologists, ethnography means "a set of methods used to collect data", and "the written record that is the product of using ethnographic techniques."[42] Merriam identifies the combination of techniques of ethnographic research, or the strategies that ethnographic researchers use in the process of data collection as being the following: "interviewing, conducting documentary analysis, examining life histories, creating investigator diaries, and observing participants."

The report of ethnographic research is the researcher's description of the data from the field. Merriam, quoting LeCompte and Preissle understands ethnography as the "researcher's reconstructions of the participants' symbolic meanings and patterns of social interaction, 'ethnographies recreate for the reader the shared beliefs, practices, artifacts, folk knowledge, and the behaviors of some groups of people.'"[43] This means that phenomena within the cultures are reported as if they are reported by researched individuals themselves. The local language of the researched area of study and its terminologies are extensively used in the research report.

However, this kind of research design requires the researcher to become familiar with social mores of the researched people. The confusion may appear if the researcher will interpret people's cultural practices from the etic perspective, i.e., from the 'outsider's point of view. In order to resolve this confusion it is necessary for the researcher to return to the field to check his/her interpretation with informants. In doing so, the researcher will validate his/her evidences before using them to support the argument in the main report.

41. Merriam, *Qualitative Research*, 14.
42. Ibid.
43. Ibid.

Doing Effective Field Work

Other Related Terms

There is something important to note. The term 'ethnography' is in most cases linked or used in place of other research terms e.g. case study, fieldwork, participant observation, and qualitative field research. Despite the fact that the terms mentioned are characteristic aspects of ethnography, no single term among them can have a complete meaning of ethnography. This is because ethnography can comprise all of those terms or some of them. This also means that ethnography does not depend on one of the terms to be accomplished, but a set of terminologies and approaches. The main issue that make ethnography ethnographic research is its concern with cultural context of a phenomenon explored, and not all studies that use fieldwork techniques are ethnographic.

Criteria for Assessing an Ethnographical Design

According to Spindler and Spindler as quoted in Creswell the following are some of the criteria for assessing an ethnographic design:

1. Observations are contextualized.
2. Hypothesis emerges in situ as the study goes on.
3. Observation is prolonged and repetitive.
4. Ethnographers elicit knowledge from informant-participants in a systematic fashion.
5. Through interviews, observations, and other eliciting procedures, the native view of reality is obtained.
6. Instruments, codes, schedules, questionnaires, agenda for interviews, and so forth are generated in situ as a result of inquiry.
7. A transcultural, comparative perspective is frequently unstated assumption.
8. The ethnographer makes explicit what is implicit and tacit to the informants.
9. The ethnographic interviewer must not predetermine responses by the kind of questions asked. [44]

Therefore, the qualitative research design which purports to be ethnographical needs to meet most of the above-outlined features.

44. Creswell, *Qualitative Inquiry*, 217–18.

Phenomenological Research Design

The third qualitative research design is phenomenological research design. Primarily, phenomenology is a philosophy through which qualitative field research draws its underpinning analytical emphasis. The term 'phenomenology' literary means a study of phenomena. Phenomenology is a way of describing things that are part of us and the world in which we live. Phenomena may be events, situations, concepts, or experiences befalling people at a given time in life in their particular places of existence.

The world we live in is populated by phenomena, and we are always surrounded by them. In most cases we fail to understand them. This luck of understanding is mainly caused by the luck of proper description. They are not clearly described for people to understand. An example may suffice to elucidate this point: we usually know that people experience loneliness in their lives; but what does loneliness really mean? We usually hear that people are compassionate to other people's anguishes; but what does the concept 'compassion' really mean? In this case, the starting point of a phenomenological study is the acknowledgement that there is a gap between the researcher's understanding and the existing phenomenon that prompts the researcher to search for meaning. The main purpose of phenomenological study is not only to bring the researcher to full understanding of studied phenomena, off course there are difficult phenomena, but also to increase awareness and insight about those phenomena.

Phenomenology emphasizes on experience as lived or perceived by a person or group of people and the interpretation they give to that experience. However, by the use of particular 'tools' of phenomenology, it is possible to conduct a phenomenological study that is slightly distinct from other qualitative studies. The study to be phenomenological, it needs to focus on "the essence or structure of an experience (phenomenon)."[45]

Quoting Patton, Merriam outlines the basic assumption of a phenomenological study: "the assumption that *there is an essence or essences to shared experience*. These essences are the core meanings mutually understood through a phenomenon commonly experienced. The experiences of different people are bracketed, analyzed, and compared to identify the essences of the phenomenon, for example, the essences of loneliness, the essence of being a mother or the essence of being a particular program. *The assumption of*

---

45. Merriam, *Qualitative Research*, 15.

essence, like the ethnographer's assumption that culture exists and is important, becomes the defining characteristic of purely phenomenological study.[46]

If the phenomenological study emphasizes on the essence or structure of an experience, what is the task of the phenomenological researcher? His/her task is "to depict the essence or basic structure of experience."[47] In order to do that, as Moustakas points out, the researcher has to capture the process required. "The process involves a blending of what is really present with what is imagined as present from the vantage point of possible meanings; thus a unity of the real and the ideal."[48]

Some criteria for assessing phenomenological design according to Pilkinghorne as quoted in Creswell are the following:[49]

1. Did the interviewer influence the contents of the participants' descriptions in such a way that the descriptions do not truly reflect the participants' actual experience?

2. Is the transcription accurate, and does it convey the meaning of the oral presentation in the interview?

3. In the analysis of the transcriptions, were there conclusions other than those offered by the researcher that could have been derived? Has the researcher identified these alternatives?

4. Is it possible to go from the general structural description to the transcriptions and to account for the specific contents and connections in the original examples of the experience?

5. Is the structural description situation specific, or does it hold in general for the experience in other situations?

Grounded Theory Research Design

The fourth qualitative field research design is grounded theory. This research design originates with Strauss and Glaser, especially in their study of the interaction between health care professionals and dying patients. In this study, as it is to all other qualitative field studies, the researcher remains the primary instrument for the collection and analysis of data. What is significant in this study is its 'end product'. A grounded theory study is designed to generate

46. Ibid (emphasis is in original).

47. Ibid, 16.

48. Mustakas in Merriam, *Qualitative Research*, 17.

49. Creswell, *Qualitative Inquiry*, 215.

"a theory that emerges from, or is grounded in, the data—hence grounded theory."[50] Hence the emphasis on generating or developing a theory to explain about an existing phenomenon is a major characteristic that distinguishes grounded theory study from other qualitative field studies. "The type of theory developed is usually 'substantive' [i.e. based on ever-day world situation and composed of categories and hypotheses derived from the study that determine the relationship among categories] rather than formal or grand theory [i.e., a theory that covers more global concerns]."[51]

Some criteria for assessing a grounded theory research design according to Straus and Gorbin as quoted in Creswell are based on the following questions:[52]

1. How was the original sample selected? What grounds?

2. What major categories emerged?

3. What were some of the events, incidents, actions, and so on (as indicators) that pointed to some of these major categories?

4. What were some of the hypotheses pertaining to conceptual relations (that is, among categories), and or what grounds were they formulated and tested?

5. Were there instances when hypotheses did not hold up against what was actually seen? How were these discrepancies accounted for? How did they affect the hypothesis?

6. How and why was the core category selected (sudden, gradual, difficult, easy)? On what grounds?

Therefore, we expect that the researcher designing a grounded theory research should meet the questions outlined above.

Case Study Research Design

The fifth qualitative field research design is case study. As the name above suggests, the main concern of case study is to work on a particular case. It is designed and used in order to "gain an in-depth understanding of the situation and meaning for those involved. The interest in process rather than outcomes, in context rather than a specific variable, in discovery rather

---

50. Merriam, *Qualitative Research*, 17.

51. Ibid.

52. Creswell, *Qualitative Inquiry*, 216.

than confirmation."[53] Robert K. Yin further elaborates: "A case study is an empirical inquiry that investigates a contemporary phenomenon in depth and within its real-life context, especially when the boundaries between phenomenon and context are not clearly evident."[54] According to Kothari, the case study "involves a careful and complete observation of a social unit, be that unit a person, a family, an institution, a cultural group or even the entire community."[55] A focus on a single unit, or a bounded system, a one unit or system out of others, is the major characteristic of case study that distinguishes it from other qualitative studies. For that matter, single units like a community, a school, a family, an organization, an event, or a person can be studied as cases.[56] The emphasis in case studies is the intensive examination of the unit under study.

There have been discussions to whether case study should be viewed as a method, a design for inquiry, or just a choice of an issue to be focused in a particular study.[57]. But in this context, I find it interesting to use it as one of the designs in qualitative field research. This is because in studying the selected issue, qualitative philosophical assumptions are quite obvious in terms of methods used and approach to the issue being studied.

Some criteria for assessing well performed case study according to Stake as quoted in Creswell are the following:[58]

1. Is the report easy to read?

2. Does it fit together, each sentence contributing to the whole?

3. Does the report have a conceptual structure (i.e. themes or issues)?

4. Are its issues developed in a serious and scholarly way?

5. Is the case adequately defined?

6. Is there a sense of story to the presentation?

7. Is the reader provided some vicarious experience?

8. Have quotations been used effectively?

53. Merriam, *Qualitative Research*, 19.

54. Yin, *Case Study Research*, 18.

55. Kothari, *Research Methodology*, 113.

56. Bryman, Social Science Research, 48–49.

57. Creswell, *Qualitative Inquiry*, 73.

58. Ibid., 218–19.

9. Are headings, figures, artefacts, appendixes, and indexes used effectively?

10. Was it edited well, then with a last minute polish?

11. Has the writer made sound assertions, neither over—nor under—interpreting?

12. Has adequate attention been paid to various contexts?

13. Were sufficient raw data presented?

14. Were data sources well chosen and in sufficient number?

15. Do observations and interpretations appear to have been triangulated?

16. Is the role and point of view of the researcher nicely apparent?

17. Is the nature of the intended audience apparent?

18. Is empathy shown for all sides?

19. Are personal intentions examined?

20. Does it appear that individuals were put at risk?

Therefore, the above listed criteria are the sole measure of the researcher's design to claim it to be a case study qualitative field research design.

Despite the distinguishing characteristics of each of the above qualitative field studies, yet they can be integrated into each other in carrying out research. This is because they share common assumptions of a qualitative field research. In terms of their distinctions, Merriam sees that the above qualitative field studies can be distinguished in terms of "disciplinary orientation (ethnography, phenomenology), function (grounded theory), or form (case study, basic or generic qualitative study)."[59] At the same time, it is possible for the qualitative studies to work together. It is possible to "conduct an ethnographic case study or a basic generic qualitative using the framework and investigative tools of phenomenology."[60]

Conclusion

The chapter has examined the 'how' question. It has discussed on the way one can carry out his/her research. It has discussed some categories of designs and the real designs of research that can be used by the researcher.

---

59. Merriam, *Qualitative Research*, 20.

60. Ibid.

Moreover, the chapter has discussed some pressing ideas of paradigm and research traditions and their role in shaping the research process. More emphasis was placed upon postmordenism and its influence to current research practice.

At the heart of the chapter are the five designs: the narrative research design, the phenomenological research design, the case study design, the grounded theory, and the ethnographical design. These designs are the essential designs in doing qualitative field researches. The chapter does not only end by just mentioning the designs but also discussing on the way to determine their ability to produce sensible and well understood research report. In this chapter, therefore, I provide the researcher with the cornerstone through which he/she can carry out research.

Moreover, the qualitative field research designs above share similar ethical responsibilities of the researcher towards his/her informants. In all the designs discussed above, the researcher deals with people in order to get the required information. In the following chapter we will deal, in a more detail, with the ethical obligation of the researcher towards safeguarding the dignity and integrity of people involved in the research process. The chapter will enlighten the researcher towards avoiding harm to participants as much as he/she can in the process of conducting his/her field research.

Chapter Highlights

1. The discussion on research design is concerned about the 'how' question. It is concerned about the way one can carry out research.

2. Research designs or ways of carrying out research are sensitive to existing traditions and paradigms. A paradigm is a cluster of beliefs that dictate the way scientists in a particular discipline have to carry out research.

3. Postmodernism is the current research paradigm. Under this paradigm, there is a shift from belief in certainties and absolute truth claims, to more localized and piecemeal factors. In this era, individuals create meaning for themselves from objects around them.

4. There are several categories of research designs in a postmodern era, three of these include: cross-section, double cross-section, and longitudinal categories.

5. The researcher decides to use a category and a design depending on the context of research and the type of data needed by that researcher. There

are five qualitative field research designs: the narrative, ethnographical, phenomenological, grounded theory, and case study designs.

Study Questions

1. Discuss the importance of designing one's own field research before commencing it.

2. What role do you think research traditions and research paradigms play in designing field research to be carried out?

3. Choose one research design among the ones discussed in this chapter and use it to design your own research project.

8

Considering Research Ethics

"Letting people know what you are studying, that you want them to participate, that their participation is voluntary, and that, if they wish, you will keep their answers confidential are important routine steps in qualitative research."

—RUBIN & RUBIN, *QUALITATIVE INTERVIEWING*, 95.

Introduction

HAVING DETERMINED A GOOD research design to use in the research process, the researcher needs to analyze and discuss sensitively the ethical issues involved in his/her research. The analysis and discussion about ethics in field research brings the researcher directly to the concern towards other people. In such a concern questions like: "How should we treat the people to whom we conduct research? Are there activities in which we should or should not engage in our relation with them?[1] In other words, what are the main ethical issues to take into account when human beings participate in the research process? These questions are important in any research where human beings are involved in a research process. They are important questions because they expose us to the dilemma befalling the decision of what is ethical and what is unethical in the conduct of research by involving human beings. It is actually

1. Bryman, *Social Science Research*, 506.

very difficult to draw a clear line between ethical and unethical aspects. What is considered ethical or unethical mainly depends on the type of problem being investigated and the context of research.

However, when human beings participate in the research process there are several general ethical issues which need to be considered: safety of research participants, informed consent from participants before embarking in the research process, trust and honesty between the researcher and his/ her participants, privacy, confidentiality and anonymity, and deception in research. These issues are our sole concern in this chapter.

Safety of Research Participants

The primary concern of the researcher in social sciences and the humanities when planning to conduct his/her field research should be to consider the safety of people who participate in the research process. This safety is partly accomplished through being careful and considerate. A researcher needs to consider the risks and benefits that participants will obtain through their active participation in the research process. An appropriate assessment using the available information regarding the status of participants in relation to the research project continuing is necessary to ensure that participants are safe from harm throughout the research process.

It is obvious that there are possible risks of harm for participants who take part in researches in social sciences and the humanities. Though it is traditionally held that medical science researches have more risks of harm for participants, social sciences and the humanities can hardly escape such possible harms to participants because they involve human beings in most of their researches. Harms resulting from participation in research are not necessarily physical. According to Miles and Huberman, harms may be social, psychological, emotional, financial, or legal. Social harm includes publishing views, opinions or attributes obtained from participants without their prior consent, hence causing participants to be embarrassed or marginalized by the communities they belong to. According to Bryman, "Harm can entail a number of facets: physical harm, harm to participants' development; loss of self-esteem; stress; and 'inducing subjects to perform reprehensible acts.'"[2]

Psychological harm may appear when the participant is deceived during the research process, or from being asked to recall or recount traumatic or difficult experiences without adequate preparation or counsel. Financial

2. Ibid., 509.

harm may happen if the participant's participation in the research may cause them to jeopardize their employment security. Legal harm may result through exploration or exposure to legal authorities because participants have accounted for a certain concealed situation involving other people in the community, and when such people are not satisfied with what the participants accounted.[3] Therefore, the researcher's involvement in ensuring the security of participants is important to consider when commencing research.

However, harm due to participation in research is not limited only to people who are researched; it cuts across both parties: the researcher and the researched. On the side of the researchers, the risk of harm can emerge if they publish something that unveils hidden issues which people are unwilling them be researched and be published. Moreover, researchers can be harmed by their informants if they publish issues that jeopardize their status in the community. In this case, it becomes important to consider who will be faced by harm in a particular study and to what extent that person or people will be harmed.

Informed Consent from Participants

The second issue to consider is informed consent from the participants. Informed consent has to do with participants in the research and their willingness to participate in a particular research project. Participants are not passive objects for investigation. They are human beings who need to have a full access to the research and its possible risks that will likely occur after their participation. Since participants are human beings, who can be vulnerable to various risks of the research results, their consent to participate is important.

Informed consent involves the provision of information to participants about what the research is all about and the possible risks that are likely to occur after or during their participation in the research project. It is also informing them about their freedom to participate or not participate in that project, their freedom to withdraw from the project at any time in the research process, and their right to be informed about the outcome of the research result.[4]

The researcher needs to obtain an informed consent from each participant, and that consent should be in writing. An oral consent can also be acceptable in some circumstances. This informed consent should be

3. Miles & Huberman, *Qualitative Data*, 292.

4. Bryman, *Social Science Research*, 511.

provided by the participant after he/she has understood all the possible benefits and risks of participating in the research. In some cases the participant can provide consent in the process of conducting research instead of before the research commences. In whatever the case, the consent needs to be soundly based on the freedom and dignity of the participant. In this case, there are four main conditions that need to be met for a sound consent: first, the competence of the participant to provide consent. In some cases, participants are not competent to provide such consent, e.g. small children, people with mental problems, seriously sick people, etc. In such cases, a close keen needs to provide consent.

Second is the voluntary and relaxed willingness of the participant. The participant needs to provide consent out of any kind of coercion, or promises of material benefits from the researcher. Third, the researcher's provision of necessary information about his/her research to the participant before such participant provides the required consent. Before the consent is provided, the participant needs to be informed fully about the nature of the research being conducted, its procedures, and how such research will be of benefit to the participant and the society at large. A full description of the research also involves the information about the way issues of confidentiality and anonymity will be handled by the researcher during and after the research process.

Fourth is the participant's comprehension of that information. The participant needs to understand what has been explained and should be provided an opportunity to inquire for what was not clear. The researcher should answer all questions asked by the participant in order to clarify what he/she has communicated to the participant about the nature of the research that the researcher plans to conduct.

Further Descriptions on Ethical Issues

Informed consent

Having provided some clues of ethical issues in the above paragraphs, we will now provide a more detailed description of these issues. We start with the question of consent provision. The participants, through understanding and signing the consent form prepared by the researcher prior to the research commencement, should provide the informed consent. The 'consent form' is a document or statement that the participant signs after having read and understood what is written in it. Researchers Herbert J. Rubin and Irene S. Rubin describe what the consent statement should contain in order to be 'informed': "An informed consent statement describes the purposes of the research, provides background on the researcher, and points out both the benefits and possible risks to those involved. It usually promises to share results with those being studied, indicates the degree of confidentiality of the findings, and most important, emphasizes that participation is fully voluntary."[5]

The above statement indicates that participants are the ones with a decisive power in their hands to participate or not participate in the research. This is because, through their acceptance to participate; they adhere to the demands and risks of the project. As Rubin and Rubin note: "Participants in a study sign these forms to show they understand the risks described in the statement and agree to be in the study."[6] In doing this signing, participants confirm that the research activity is also their own. They confirm it to be a relational activity, a mutual relational activity between the researcher and participants from whom information is sought.

Informed consent is part of every research. This is what Rubin and Rubin remind us when they emphasize on informed consent in qualitative researches: "Letting people know what you are studying, that you want them to participate, that their participation is voluntary, and that, if they wish, you will keep their answers confidential are important routine steps in qualitative research."[7]

However, it should be clearly known, that, informed consent and signing a consent statement are not without effect to the research process. In most cases, providing information to participants about the research can be puzzling to them, hence leading to superficial research results.[8] In some situations, signing a consent form as a means of acceptance to participate may be something unknown to participants.[9]

In other situations and types of topics, excessive freedom of participants to participate in the research may lead to no participant at all, and hence no any research being done in such topics. In such cases, I would advise that informed consent needs to be a contextual issue. Matters relating to informed consent need to be handled according to a particular situation and a particular context. A good example of handling such issues

---

5. Rubin & Rubin, *Qualitative Interviewing*, 95.

6. Ibid.

7. Ibid.

8. Ibid., cf. Mligo, *Jesus and the Stigmatized*, 28–29.

9. Cf. Mligo, *Jesus and the Stigmatized*, 28–29.

is debriefing whereby the information is withheld at the beginning of the research process and debriefed later in the process.

Problems with informed consent may also arise when considering to whom one has to provide the consent for the study. Doing researches among people in an institution may be problematic especially when the consent is to be provided by the superior person of that organization. It may mean coercing the subordinates to participate, which may further imply that the information they provide should serve the purpose of the superior person in that institution.[10] For example, doing research among children, whose consent has to be provided by their parents or guardians may mean coercing them to participate, and their information should serve the purpose of their parents or guardians.

Another problem may arise when considering the amount of information needed to be provided to participants about the project prior to the commencement of the research process.[11] How much detail requires to be provided about the design, purpose or consequences of the research in order for participants to understand the project before they sign the consent form? I argue elsewhere that, in most cases, signing a consent form hardly guarantees that participants have understood the description of the consent statement. Participants may sign the consent statement for different purposes from those intended by the researcher.[12] And sometimes, too much information about the project, especially its specific purpose, may lead them to providing direct answers to the questions posed to them. The signing of a consent statement without understanding and the direct answers they will provide both lead to superficial data that eventually lead to superficial research report.[13]

Honesty and Trust Between the Researcher and Participants

The third issue that the researcher should consider involves the questions of honesty and trust between him/her and the participants in the research. Is there truth and sincerity in their communication? Has the researcher spoken the truth about the purpose and nature of research to the research participants? In most cases, the honesty and trust of the researcher upon

10. Kvale & Brinkmann, *Interviews*, 71.

11. Ibid.

12. Mligo, *Jesus and the Stigmatized*, 28–29.

13. Kvale & Brinkmann, *Interviews*, 72.

his/her participants determine their honesty and trust, and their willingness to provide reliable information.[14]

Privacy, Confidentiality, and Anonymity

The fourth issues to consider in research with human participants are privacy, confidentiality and anonymity. Miles and Huberman have defined the above confusing terms as follows: "Privacy: control over others' access to oneself and associated information; preservation of boundaries against giving protected information or receiving unwanted information. Confidentiality: agreements with a person or organization about what will be done (and may not be done) with their data; may include legal constraints. Anonymity: lack of identifiers, information that would indicate which individuals or organizations provide which data."[15]

The privacy of the informant entails his/her self and what he/she has (information) as something private and secret. The researcher needs to recognize that entering the world of the informant in order to explore his/her potential information is attempting to know someone's secret and private information. In this case, the information obtained needs to be handled carefully in such a way that the status of the informant is not subjected to jeopardy. On the other hand, issues of confidentiality and anonymity are agreements between the researcher and the informants that control their possibility to be identified in the report. In these issues, the informant agrees with the researcher on matters of the way raw data and analyses will be stored, and the way the data and analyses will be handled after they are collected.

Deception in Research

Deception occurs when the researcher decides to report things that are not so in the research location. In most cases this happens because the researcher has not done research or the research done did not provide him/her sufficient data to help him/her argue a case. In other incidences the researcher, because of the constraints of the requirements at a college or faculty and his/her lack of enough time to conduct research, may decide to sit at table and produce data from his/her own head without the knowledge

14. Miles & Huberman, *Qualitative Data*, 292.
15. Ibid., 293.

of any field location. This is typical deception. The researcher deceives not only the institution where he/she submits the research report, but also the audience that will read the written report. Therefore deception takes several malevolent forms including the ones mentioned above.

In fact, it is very difficult to identify deception and real research when the report is presented to a certain college or faculty. Research is the matter of trust to the part of the institution that receives the report because none of the institutional members were there when the researcher conducted his/her research. It is also the matter of honesty to the part of the researcher knowing that cheating is the enemy of science. However, most supervisors have tried to visit the research area where the student conducts research in order to verify the research activities of the students. This has also not been effective because this supervisor cannot be there in the whole process of collecting data. Therefore, the knowledge about the reliability of data collected from the field is upon the researcher himself/herself. This reliability depends mainly on the expertise of the researcher, the type of problem dealt with and the instrument used for data collection.

Research Clearance

The obligation to the researcher to follow research ethics means that the researcher has to do clearance about his/her research to be carried out. This clearance requires that the research designed comply to the laws on conducting research within a particular country. In Tanzania, for example, research clearance is granted by the government and the Tanzania Commission for Science and Technology.[16]

Research clearance is important because it ensures the safety of participants and of the area where research is to be conducted. It also provides a particular researcher with a permission to proceed with research in a particular area of study. It also ensures that the design, and methodology employed do not jeopardize the statuses of the individuals involved and the area where such research is planned to be conducted. Therefore, carrying out research clearance is important for all researches in order to be legitimate and safe.

16. Ndunguru, *Lectures on Research*, 59.

Conclusion

Research participants are human beings like any other human being. They need respect and honor worth of any human being. When the researcher approaches participants to inquire for information, he/she interrupts the privacy of that person. Under this situation, questions concerning the rights and freedom of participants are inevitable. The rights and freedom of participants to participate or not participate in the research need to be respected. The freedom of participants to provide consent or not to provide, the rights of participants to be protected from any harm, the freedom of participants to withdraw from the research process are issues to be taken into account. The participants are not supposed to participate in research through any kind of cohesion. This chapter has concerned itself in such kind of ethical issues.

Generally this chapter has concentrated on the above stated ethical guidelines that enable the researcher to protect his/her participants from physical and psychological harm in order to make his/her participants be safe. Participants do not need to encounter any kind of harm in virtue of the information they provide. This protection of participants from harm can be possible through practicing the ethical guidelines: informed consent, confidentiality, honesty and trust, privacy, anonymity, and avoiding deception. In this case, this chapter has argued that ethics of research are extremely important for researchers to adhere to if they are to do justice to the dignity and integrity of research participants.

Chapter Highlights

1. Participants of field research process have the freedom to participate or not participate in the research. When the researcher requests participants to participate, he/she interrupts the freedom and privacy of those participants. In this case, questions about the freedom and privacy of participants need to be addressed.

2. One of the most crucial things to consider in the research process is obtaining an informed consent from participants. The researcher may obtain this consent before commencing the research or within the process.

3. The researcher needs to handle carefully all issues pertaining to confidentiality, honesty and trust, and anonymity.

Study Questions

1. Discuss the importance of informed consent from participants before embarking into research with them.

2. Discuss the meaning of the following terms as used in research ethics: honesty, deception, confidentiality, privacy, anonymity, trust, and plagiarism.

3. Why do you think research clearance is important before conducting research in a certain field of study?

9

Selecting Instruments for Data Collection

"The construction of a research instrument or tool is the most important aspect of a research project because anything you say by way of findings or conclusions is based upon the type of information you collect, and the data you collect is entirely dependant upon the questions that you ask of your respondents."

—KUMAR, *RESEARCH METHODOLOGY*, 137.

Introduction

HAVING UNDERSTOOD THE ETHICAL obligations regarding the participants of research, the field researcher needs to select a suitable instrument to help him/her collect the needed data. Regarding the collection of data, Vyhmeister directs the field researcher thus: "After you know exactly what the problem to be solved is, you can begin collecting data. Gather information carefully from many sources. Organize your data in a way that is clear and logical to you and to others."[1] Following the above directive, this chapter introduces to the field researcher the various instruments that can be used in collecting qualitative field data, and their advantages and disadvantages. We argue in this chapter that the type of instruments used depends sorely on the type of data which the field researcher needs to col-

1. Vyhmeister, *Quality Research Papers*, 3.

lect. This means that the instruments used in the data collection process depend mainly on two main approaches: whether the field researcher needs to collect *primary* or *secondary* data. These two approaches determine what is the *method (or instrument)* for data collection should be used and the *sources* one will use in his/her data collection process. In principle, primary data are collected from primary sources and secondary data are collected from secondary sources.

Gall, Borg and Gall define primary and secondary sources for data collection as follows: "A *secondary source* is a document written by someone who did not actually do the research, develop the theories, or express the opinions that they have synthesized into the literature review. . . . A *primary source* is a document (e.g. journal article, or dissertation) that was written by individuals who actually conducted the research study or who formulated the theory or opinions that are described in the document."[2] Following the above definitions, all data that are gathered by the field researcher from the field through qualitative or quantitative methods of data collection are primary data, while data gathered by other researchers and are used by the field researcher in order to substantiate his/her argument are secondary data.

Collecting Primary Data

What is primary data? Primary data is research information obtained from firsthand informers, and secondary data is research information obtained from second hand informers. However, field researchers believe that none of the methods, whether one used to collect primary data or the one used to collect secondary data, is a hundred percent the best method for researchers to get accurate and reliable information about phenomena, people, or issues they research. In this case, the sensibility of the field researcher, whether experienced or amateur, towards factors that can affect the quality of data obtained during his/her research is an important rudiment.[3]

What is an instrument in data collection, and why is it important in research? Ranjit Kumar notes that "Anything that becomes a means of collecting information for your study is called a 'research instrument."[4] Examples of such instruments include: the field researcher himself/herself, "observation

2. Gall, Borg & Gall, *Educational Research*, 117 (emphasis is in original).

3. Ibid., 118–19.

4. Ibid., 22.

forms, interview schedules questionnaires and interview guides (. . .)."[5] We discuss some of the qualitative research instruments below.

The instrument of collecting data is a very important tool in research because it indicates how the field researcher will obtain data for his/her problem. The method part of the research report indicates to the readers the way the field researcher got the results in his/her research process. There are several reasons why readers would be interested to know how the field researcher got the data. Some of these reasons are:

First, the way the researcher collects data greatly determines the quality of the results obtained. Every instrument is useful for particular questions and situations. In this case, the reader of the research report will be able to evaluate the validity and reliability of the research results if he/she knows the instrument that the researcher used in collecting them.

Second, since methods for data collection are numerous and the researcher is free to select or design any method to use for his/her purpose, then, the reader of the report will be interested to see the reasons for selecting to use the method for that particular research process. The reader will assess the plausibility of the reasons provided based on the results reported. In this case, the researcher is obliged to provide clear and persuasive reasons why he/she selected to use a particular instrument for data collection.

Third, since every field of study, say sociology, theology, medicine, mathematics, etc., has peculiar ways of collecting data, and that most of the readers of the report will be from the researcher's field of study, then, the readers will be interested in ways through which the researcher's instrument selected is consistent with the generally accepted practice at that particular field. The researcher is, therefore, obliged to be sensitive to the way research is practiced in his/her field of study.

Fourth, the main intention or objective of the study will determine the type of instrument the researcher selects to use. Since it is possible that the researcher can have a particular objective, very genuine one, yet select an inappropriate instrument to execute his/her objective, then the reader of the report will be interested to know whether the instrument used to collect data is appropriate to the objectives stated.

Fifth, if it is a new instrument, i.e., an instrument that the researcher has designed and has just introduced to the field, the reader of the report will be interested to know if there is a possibility of using the instrument in another situation of a similar category. In this way, the researcher needs to

5. Ibid.

provide clear, and sufficient information to enable other researchers to use the instrument for further research.

Collecting Secondary Data

What are secondary data? Secondary data are data collected by other researchers. These data aim at answering their own questions at their times and in their own contexts of research. Every research begins with the analysis of secondary data. The analysis of secondary data determines the need to collect primary data regarding the problem of research. This is, in most cases, what it means by engaging in literature review before carrying out a new research about a particular topic. Literature review makes it possible to analyze the existing data and theories they support in order to determine the gap of knowledge that prompts the researcher to embark in a new research.[6]

However, there is a difference between literature review and secondary data analysis. In literature review, as we have just said, the researcher makes a survey about the existing gap of knowledge. In secondary data analysis the researcher engages in an in-depth study of the data trying to analyze and come out with a new understanding and expression of the phenomenon. In most cases, secondary data analysis is done by researchers who decide to use only secondary data for their analysis according to the nature of their studies. Therefore, such kind of researchers need to make a clear distinction on what is literature review and what is secondary data analysis in order not to confuse between the two aspects.[7]

Some advantages and disadvantages of secondary data according to Wilson are the following:[8]

Disadvantages of Secondary Data

(i) They may be outdated. This mainly depends on what type of environment are the data collected. The data may be relevant but very old. Since they are very old, they cannot provide the account of what the researcher is trying to find out in his/her current time. Therefore, the researcher may

6. For more about secondary data see Wilson, *Essentials of Business Research*, 167–87.

7. Wilson, *Essentials of Business Research*, 174.

8. Ibid., 177–79.

run the risk of reporting things which are contrary to what is going on in his/her contemporary situation.

(ii) It is difficult to determine their reliability. Reliability always depends on the type of source used.

(iii) Access to some of this data is costly, especially those data associated with sensitive issues pertaining the government and communities.

(iv) Most of this data may not match the researcher's research concerns. This means that it costs the researcher's time and energy to search for secondary data that are relevant to his/her research concerns.

Advantages of Secondary Data

(i) They are less resource intensive. Since they can be available in published sources, it is very easy to access them via libraries or stores without much expense.

(ii) They can be compared to the researcher's findings (i.e. primary findings). In doing this, the researcher can agree or disagree with the existing data.

(iii) They can save time and energy of the researcher because they do not oblige the researcher to go to the real place where they were collected.

The Researcher as a Primary Instrument

In qualitative field studies, the researcher plays the first role as an instrument of data collection and analysis. This is because his ability to perceive meanings embedded in phenomena, issues and situations is important as he/she comes in contact with people. Steinar Kvale and Svend Brinkmann state, "When the person of the researcher becomes the main research instrument, the competence and craftsmanship—the skills, sensitivity, and knowledge—of the researcher become essential for the quality of the knowledge produced."[9] Since the researcher is a primary instrument in the two tasks (collection and analysis of data), he/she has the ability to respond to the situation in the field in a way that enhances or minimizes the opportunity to get ostensible information from his/her informants. However, the researcher is a human being, and hence, vulnerable to limitations. As a human being, he/she is limited to a number of aspects in the process

9. Kvale & Brinkmann, *Interviews*, 84.

of collecting data: "mistakes are made, opportunities are missed, personal biases interfere."[10] In this case, the researcher's fallibility in the process of research indicates his/her creatureliness and the unavoidable vulnerability to weakness for all creatures.

Merriam outlines three qualities of the researcher as a primary instrument of data collection and analysis: tolerance for ambiguity, sensitivity, and being a good communicator. Qualitative research is naturally ambiguous because it does not have structured set of procedures to follow step by step when conducting research. Merriam states this clearly when she writes: "Throughout the research process—from designing the study, to data collection, to data analysis—there are no set procedures or protocols that can be followed step by step."[11] This means that always the qualitative researcher will have to find out the way which is suitable to carry out his/her research.

However, "The very lack of structure is what makes this type of research appealing to many, for it allows the researcher to adopt the unforeseen events and change direction in pursuit of meaning."[12] In this sense, though qualitative research lacks structured procedures or protocols, yet allows for the researcher's flexibility depending on the context, situation and type of people he/she finds in the field.

The question of sensitivity of the researcher in qualitative research involves the way the researcher perceives his/her context of study and its existing variables. The more sensitive and able to handle meanings of variables and context, the more meaningful data the researcher will obtain. The researcher needs to be sensitive to "the physical setting, the people, the overt and covert agendas, and the nonverbal behaviour. The researcher must be sensitive to the information being gathered. What does it reveal? How can it lead to the next peace of data? How well does it reflect what is happening? (. . .) the researcher must be aware of any personal biases and how they may influence the investigation."[13] The researcher also needs to be sensitive to recognize the 'saturation point' of his data gathered during the data gathering point. The 'saturation point' is the point when no new information is obtained in the researcher's investigation process.

10. Merriam, *Qualitative Research*, 20.

11. Ibid.

12. Ibid., 20–21.

13. Ibid., 21.

Despite the above two qualities of the qualitative researcher, tolerance for ambiguity and sensitivity to variables and contexts, the researcher also requires to be 'a good communicator'. According to Merriam, "a good communicator empathizes with respondents, establishes rapport, asks good questions and listens intently."[14] These are aspects of empathy, which is a very important entity of a good communicator.

Why is empathy so important aspect for a qualitative researcher who is a good communicator? This is important partly because of the nature of sources for his/her data. Most of the sources for qualitative data are human beings and what they experience. The researcher needs an approach to fellow human beings that allows them to freely provide information to the researcher about what they experience and the meaning of that experience. People have information in their minds which the researcher needs to explore. "Since what is in and on someone's mind cannot be directly observed or measured, the interviewer [researcher] has to ask questions in such a way as to obtain meaningful information."[15] In order for the researcher to do that he/she needs to empathize with the informants and build an environment of trust, aspects that will build good rapport with his/her informants.

Communication involves listening and speaking. Speaking can be verbal or nonverbal. The qualitative researcher as a good communicator must have a 'big ear' to listen and a 'small mouth' to talk. Merriam writes that "The good qualitative researcher 'looks and listens everywhere.' It is by listening 'to many individuals and to many points of view that value-resonant social contexts can be fully, equitably, and honourably represented.'"[16] As stated earlier, the researcher also needs to hear tacit communications from his/her informants. "'Hearing' what is not explicitly stated but only implied, as well as noting the silences, whether in interviews, observations, or documents, is an important component of being a good listener."[17]

Interviews as an Instrument

Meaning of Interview

The use of 'interviews' as an instrument for collecting qualitative data is not something strange in qualitative research. The aim of qualitative

14. Ibid., 27.
15. Ibid., 23.
16. Ibid.
17. Ibid.

interviewing is getting meaningful information from the sample of informants selected by the researcher. The information that the researcher wants to explore is concerned with the informants' experiences of the world around them; they are concerned with how the informants understand their world and their lives. As Irving Seidman puts it, "At the root of in-depth interviewing is an interest in understanding the lived experience of other people and the meaning they make of that experience."[18] This experience is within the informants' minds and the researcher strives to explore this experience. In this case, interviewing is entering into the worldview of the informants, the worldview enshrined in their minds, in order to understand it.

Types of Questions to Ask

Knowing or understanding the worldview of informants becomes possible through questioning to explore what is enshrined in their minds. In order for the researcher to better achieve this goal, he/she needs to ask 'good questions' and recognize well his/her role in the interview process. Merriam categories four types of good questions which the interviewer can use in his/her interview sessions: hypothetical, devil advocate, ideal, and interpretive questions.[19]

According to Merriam, hypothetical questions are speculative about the future. Asking speculative questions is asking the informants to say something that can possibly happen in the future according to their views. Such questions start with "What if . . . " or "Suppose . . . "[20] These questions imagine a hypothetical situation that the informants will have to describe their responses.

Harry F. Walcott also outlines six guidelines that can lead the researcher perform better interviews: The researcher should regard oneself more as a listener and not as a speaker, the researcher should listen more, and speak less, the researcher should make his questions to informants short and to the point, the researcher should plan the interviews around a big issue and should be focused to that planned issue, the researcher should write up the notes of what he/she heard as soon as the interview is completed, the

18. Seidman, *Interviewing*, 9.

19. Merriam, *Qualitative Research*, 77.

20. Ibid.

researcher should discuss before hand what type of interview to be conducted: semi-structured, structured, or unstructured.[21]

There are times when the researcher will have to explore the views of participants about a particular controversial issue. At this point, he/she will have to use devils advocate questions to accomplish his/her goal. Such types of questions mean to explore "respondents' opinions and feelings."[22] They usually begin with "Some people would say . . . " whose response will be about the way the respondents fell or have opinions about the issue.[23]

Ideal questions inquire for an ideal situation according to the opinion of the informants. In this case, such questions "elicit both information and opinion" from the informants about the ideal nature of the inquired issue.[24]

Interpretative questions are used when the researcher knows something about what he/she inquires. His/her aim in asking such questions is to prove his knowledge, or to get more information from informants about the issue. In this case, the interpretive question mentions the issue in order to get a positive or negative response from the informants. For example, would you say that being an HIV–positive in your society is stigmatized? This question proves the knowledge of the researcher and also can add new information from what he/she already knows.

In asking all the questions discussed above, the researcher should use the everyday language commonly known to the participants. He/she should avoid all jargons and professional terminologies that are not understood by informants. This is because doing so will hinder informants to provide adequate data.[25]

However, Merriam warns that there are questions that are bad and unworthy asking. The researcher should not ask "multiple questions", i.e., questions that comprise more than one question in a single question. For example, how do you feel about pastors and HIV positive persons in your society? This question has two questions: the informant has to provide his/her feelings about pastors, then about HIV persons. The question may be difficult to the informant to provide adequate responses to both questions that are meaningful to the purposes of the researcher. This is because the respondent will ask for clarification, ask for the question to be repeated,

21. Walcott, *The Art of Fieldwork*, 111–13.

22. Merriam, *Qualitative Research*, 77.

23. Ibid.

24. Ibid., 78.

25. Kumar, *Research Methodology*, 135.

respond to one part of it or respond superficially to both.[26] There can be no in-depth response to two or more questions asked in a single question.

The researcher also needs to avoid asking "leading questions." These questions "reveal a bias or an assumption that the researcher is making, which may not be held by the participants."[27] An example of leading questions is this: What bad reaction did you have after your parents chased you out of home? The informant might have no any bad reaction after the event. But the informant may respond following the bias of the researcher who thinks there was a 'bad reaction' after the chasing. This type of questions hinders the informants from exploring their potentials about the issue at hand.

Other dangerous questions that need to be avoided are those requiring a 'Yes' and 'No' answers. These are dangerous because they hinder the exploration of the information inscribed in the informant's mind. Examples of such questions include: Do you believe in science as a way to understand the world? Do you accept that religion is opium of the people? However, such questions can be rephrased in order for them to explore for more information from the informants. For example: Some people believe in science as a way to understand the world, what is your opinion about that? What is your opinion to the assertion that religion is the opium of the people? These rephrased questions explore the opinion of the respondent instead of allowing him/her to simply respond 'yes' or 'no'.[28]

The types of questions to avoid applies to all questions: main questions that are characteristic of structured interviews, and main questions, probing questions, and follow-up questions that are characteristic of semi-structured and unstructured interviews. *Probes* are questions asked following the respondent's answer to the main question. Its main purpose is to explore the information beyond what the respondent has just provided in his/her response to the main question. Herbert J. Rubin and Irene S. Rubin explain about probing questions more clearly: "Probes perform three functions in interview. First, they help specify the level of depth the interviewer wants. Probes signal the interviewees that you want longer and more detailed answers, specific examples, or evidence. Probes encourage the speaker to keep elaborating. Second, probes ask the interviewee to finish up the particular answer currently being provided. The interviewer may ask the interviewee to clarify an ambiguity or fill in missing information

26. Merriam, *Qualitative Research*, 78.
27. Ibid., 78–79 cf. Kumar, *Research Methodology*, 135.
28. Merriam, *Qualitative Research*, 79.

necessary to understand the answer. The third function of probes is to indicate that the interviewer is paying attention."[29]

Rubin and Rubin further elaborate on the types of probes: 'attention probes' that indicate that the researcher is interested with what the interviewee has just said and would like him/her to continue elaborating, 'continuation probes' that signal the interviewee that what he/she says is right on target and encourage him/her to keep on elaborating, 'clarification probes' that need more elaboration in order to make the point more clear, and 'evidence probes' that require the interviewee to provide an evidence in order to substantiate a particular point just stated.[30]

It should be remembered that there is no one way of probing. The way of probing depends greatly on the issue explored and what the researcher aspires to know from his/her informants. What can be said here is that probing questions are emergent and situational. In addition to questions, a probe may be a comment about the informant's response that provides more room for the informant to provide further information. In most cases, this comment does not leave the informant content with it; he/she has to respond to it. Therefore, probing questions that are well-framed and asked curiously, can help the researcher acquire more information from the informants apart from the one he/she obtains from the response to the main question.

The researcher makes a follow-up of the issue to explore its details as understood by the informants. This is also stated more clearly in Rubin and Rubin: "The purpose of follow-up questions is to get the depth that is hallmark of (. . .) interviewing by pursuing themes that are discovered, elaborating the context of answers, and exploring the implications of what has been said."[31] In this case, through probing and follow-up questions asked, the researcher's being a primary instrument for data collection becomes visible.

Types of Interviews

In qualitative research, interviews are divided into three depending on the way questions are asked: highly structured, semi-structured and unstructured interviews. *Highly structured interviews* are those whose questions are pre-determined by the researcher before the interview session begins and

29. Rubin & Rubin, *Qualitative Interviewing*, 148 cf. Bryman, *Social Science Research*, 122–23.

30. Ibid., 148–50.

31. Ibid., 151.

the data obtained depends mainly on the way informants understand and answer those questions. This means that the more understood are the questions the more likely will the researcher get sufficient responses, and vice versa. Moreover, the more information the researcher gets the better for his/her research. There is no other question added to the pre-determined questions. Therefore, the highly structured interview questions are re-searcher-centered. They are prepared by the researcher, and the informants will provide data depending on those questions. There will be neither addition nor reduction of data expected from the informants. The researcher is the determinant of what data should informants provide.

The advantage of this type of interview is that its questions will be thought about thoroughly before asking and so minimizing the possibility of asking bad questions. Another advantage is that the questions are specific to what the researcher wants to know, and do not allow any kind of meandering or running around the issue under investigation. The serious disadvantage of such interview, however, is that such kind of structured questions it uses cannot explore more information from the informants apart from that required from the questions. In this case, this type of interview runs the risk of leaving more potential information unexplored, a thing that can lead the researcher acquiring less information from the informants about the phenomenon than he expected, especially if the questions will not be clearly understood by the informants.[32]

The second type of qualitative interviews is *semi-structured interviews*. This stands in between structured and open ended or unstructured interviews. It contains questions that are structured but allows for *probes* within the interview session. The formulation of structured questions allows for further exploration of the investigator through probes. The important advantage of this type of interview is that it allows the investigator to get the most important information he/she needs through the structured question, yet allowing him/her to make follow-ups for unclear aspects of the information provided by the informant.[33]

The third type of qualitative interviews is the *open-ended* or *unstructured interviews*. In this type of interview, context provides to the researcher questions to be asked. It is mostly used when the researcher does not know very well what will be the relevant questions to ask his/her informants in a particular context of research. The advantage of unstructured interview is that it

32. Merriam, *Qualitative Research*, 73–74.
33. Ibid., 74.

allows the researcher to explore as much information as possible through his/her own creativity. It also provides a great room for the researcher's flexibility to the on-going interview process in favor of gaining more meaningful data.[34]

However, there are some problems with this type of interview: since there is no plan of what to ask and what not, it is possible for the interview to get lost. The researcher can fail to focus to what is important leading him/her to collecting a large amount of meaningless information regarding his/her phenomenon of investigation. Despite this weakness, this type of interview is highly recommended when the researcher does some participant observations, especially in early stages of ethnography as the researcher strives to become acquainted with the field.[35]

According to Kumar unstructured interviews are further sub-divided into the following categories: in-depth, focus group, narrative and oral histories unstructured interviews.[36] Let us discuss each of these categories in a more detail.

In-depth interviews: According to Taylor and Bogdan, in-depth interview is a "repeated face-to-face encounters between the researcher and informants directed towards understanding informants' perspectives on their lives, experiences, or situations as expressed in their own words (. . .)."[37] According to Kumar, two characteristics of this type of unstructured interview are obvious. First, "it involves face-to-face, repeated interaction between the researcher and his/her informants" and second, "it seeks to understand the latter's perspectives."[38] In most cases, this type of unstructured interviews takes place with a single informant being involved in the interview. Hence, the quality of data that the researcher gets from his/her informant in this type of unstructured interview will greatly depend on the rapport the researcher maintains during the interview sessions.

Focus Group interviews: In focus group interviews, a group of people is involved in the interview session. Instead of exploring the perceptions, understandings and experiences of a phenomenon or situation by a single informant (as done in in-depth interviews), here the researcher explores how the whole group understands, perceives and experiences the phenomenon, situation, or issue under investigation.

---

34. Ibid., 75.
35. Ibid, cf. Kumar, *Research Methodology*, 125.
36. Kumar, *Research Methodology*, 24.
37. Taylor and Bogdan in Kumar, *Research Methodology*, 124.
38. Kumar, *Research Methodology*, 125.

What is a focus group? Roseline Barbour, quoting Kitzinger and Barbour, lays out a definition of a focus group. According to her, "Any group discussion may be called focus group as long as the researcher is actively encouraging, and attentive to, the group interaction."[39] This means that the researcher has to facilitate the group discussions. In his/her facilitation process the researcher should ensure that "participants talk among themselves rather than interacting with the researcher, or 'moderator.'"[40] The information recorded should be the result of the informants' interaction with one another within the group, and not their interaction with the researcher. In this type of unstructured interview, the researcher's role in facilitating the process is very important to determine the interview success.

In order to succeed in attaining a proper understanding, "broad discussion topics are developed beforehand, either by the researcher or by the group."[41] The data of this type of unstructured interview is the various opinions expressed during the discussion process. What the researcher needs to bear in mind is how such opinions are recorded. The better the recording, the more accurate will be the information. There are several ways for doing that: audio taping, employing someone to record the ongoing discussions or the researcher's taking of his/her own notes of what he/or she hears from the informants. However, each of the above ways of capturing data has its own advantages and disadvantages that are important for the researcher to be aware and try to handle them accordingly.

Narrative interviews: This is also called 'storytelling'. The main purpose of the researcher in this type of unstructured interview is to hear the personal experience as narrated or told by the informant. It is mostly used in exploring situations that are sensitive, e.g., sexual abuses, racist experiences, etc. The researcher asks the informant(s) to tell their experiences or perceptions of the situations or phenomena. In this type of unstructured interviews, the researcher is more a 'listener' in the process and the informants are the 'speakers'. Through this listening (the researcher) and speaking (the informants), narrative interviewing can be a place for healing for informants with hurting experiences of situations or phenomena apart from being places for research.

However, for the researcher to explore maximum information from the informants, he/she needs to encourage, or motivate the informants to

39. Barbour, *Doing Focus Groups*, 2.

40. Ibid.

41. Kumar, *Research Methodology*, 124.

continue narrating their stories. This can be done by using words like 'oh yes', 'uh huh', 'ok', 'really!' 'wonderful', 'mmmm', 'right', nodding the head, or any other body gesture that will motivate the informant to freely continue narrating about his/her life experience.[42] Again, recording of data is a crucial thing to consider. Similar methods of capturing data as those with focus group interviews can be used in this type of unstructured interview.

Oral Histories: - This is similar to narratives type discussed above. Their difference is mainly on their interests: While narratives interviewing is interested in hearing the informant(s) story about the experience on a phenomenon at the time the researcher conducts research, oral histories focus on hearing the experience of the informant(s) about a historical event, an episode that took place sometime in the past. Events like the Arab's slave trade, a particular cultural practice or custom that was effective in the past can be learned by the researcher. In learning this, the researcher will have to identify informants that are knowledgeable about them and let them tell stories about them. These persons might be the ones who were alive that time, or are in one way or another more knowledgeable about them.[43]

Advantages and Disadvantages of Interviews

Kumar lists advantages and disadvantages of using interviews as an instrument for data collection. [44]

Advantages of Interviews

1. The interview is more appropriate for complex situations: Since interview is an encounter between the researcher and the informants, it is a good instrument for studying sensitive and more complex issues. The researcher has the opportunity to prepare his/her interview participants before the meeting time and ask them sensitive questions in person.

2. It is useful for collecting in-depth information: In-depth information is mostly obtained through the researcher's endeavor to probe beneath what he/she hears from the informants. Since the researcher meets

---

42. Kumar, *Research Methodology*, 124–25.

43. Ibid., 125.

44. Kumar, *Research Methodology*, 131–32.

informants in person, he/she has the opportunity to ask probing questions for deeper understanding of the phenomenon under investigation.

3. Information can be supplemented: In most qualitative researches, interviews are used together with the researcher's observations of what is going on in the field. By supplementing interview data, it means that the researcher's understanding of the interview information can be supplemented with the information the researcher gets from observation or tacit knowledge gained from the way informants non-verbally react towards the researcher.

4. Questions can be explained: During the session, the researcher encounters the informants in person and asks questions. This provides an opportunity for clarifying the questions asked in case they are not clearly understood by the informant. Clarification can be done by repeating the asked question as it is, or rephrasing it in a better understood way.

5. Interviewing has a wider application: The wider application implied here is the 'Whom and What' (informants, phenomena and situations) can this instrument be applicable. The instrument can be applicable to a wide range of groups of people, and yet be successful. It can be used to explore about various phenomena, highly sensitive and less sensitive. It can also be used to a variety of situations. Some of the groups or populations that this instrument can be used include: the youth, the children, women, men, old people, learned, unlearned, and people with body impairments.

Disadvantages of Interviews

1. Interviewing is time consuming and expensive: The interviewer becomes involved in the process in most of his/her time. He/she has to arrange everything and accomplish it till the end of the interview process. This becomes costly if the interviews are conducted to informants that are far from the researcher's residence, and if such informants are scattered.

2. The quality of data depends on the quality of the interaction: In interviews the researcher has the prerogative to influence the quality of data obtained. His/her approach and interaction with informants determines greatly the data he/she will obtain. If the researcher maintains a good empathy and rapport, it is possible to influence informants to be open and freely provide the required data, and vice versa. In this case, the quality of every interview is unique and depends on the interaction between the researcher and the informants.

3. The quality of data depends on the quality of the interviewer: Here what is emphasized is the experience of the researcher. A novice interviewer can hardly produce good quality data due to insufficient skills for maintaining rapport in the process. Inexperienced interviewers can hardly know the type of questions to ask and which not to ask, which to probe for more information and which not in a particular phenomenon, situation or issue under investigation. In this case, combining all these issues in pursuit of acquiring information requires experience.

4. The quality of data may vary when many interviewers are used. This means that if more than one interviewer is used to research the issue to a single informant, it is possible that each will get information that is different from the other ones. This is because, as described in disadvantage number three above, the experiences of the interviewers are not the same. Each one of them will have an approach and rapport different from the others.

5. The researcher may introduce his/her bias. By introducing the researcher's bias here it means that the researcher may frame the questions that favor the type of response he/she wishes. This can be done knowingly or unknowingly. The researcher can also show his/her biases in the interpretation of the responses provided.

6. The researcher may be biased. This refers not only to the questions where the researcher can 'introduce' his/her bias, but to the whole process. The researcher can be biased in his/her selection of the interview sample, interpretation of responses, selection of categories from data, and even in reporting the findings. It is possible to neglect or not to see the main opinion of the informants. All this can happen because the interviewer or researcher is a primary instrument in the process.

Observation as an Instrument

To observe issues happening around is part and parcel of human life. Any human being, born normal, can perceive, interpret and evaluate what is happening around him/her through his/her observation. In doing that consciously or unconscious, the human being becomes a natural observer of his/her everyday world while making sense out of what he/she sees. However, despite the fact that the human being is a natural observer of the world around him/her, yet that does not mean that every observation is *research*.

Merriam, quoting Kidder identifies four aspects of observation that is credited as being research. According to him: "Observation is a *research* tool when it '(1) serves a formulated research purpose, (2) is planned de-liberately, (3) is recorded systematically, and (4) is subjected to checks and controls on validity and reliability."[45] Therefore, the observation with the above qualities is a very useful tool for collecting qualitative primary data.

As it has been clearly noted by Merriam above, "Observation is a purposeful, systematic and selective way of watching and listening to an interaction or phenomenon as it takes place."[46] Observation is dif-ferent from interviews as tools for collecting primary data. Merriam distinguishes two of these differences: "First, observations take place in the natural field setting instead of a location designed for the purpose of interviewing; second, observational data represent a first hand encounter with the phenomenon of interest rather than a second hand account of the world obtained in an interview."[47]

Why use observation as a tool for collecting data? This question is crucial before one selects interview as his/her instrument for collecting field data. Some of the reasons for this question are the following: First, "As an outsider an observer will [or wants to] notice things that have become routine to the participants themselves, things that may lead to understand-ing the context."[48] This observation enables the researcher to see things as they happen and use his/her skills and knowledge to make sense of what has been observed. Second, in cases where interviews are used together with observations, observation can serve "to provide some knowledge of the context or to provide specific incidents, behaviors and so on that can be used as reference points for subsequent interviews."[49]

What should the researcher observe in the research field? In a none re-search observation, of course, the researcher can observe everything he/she sees in the field. But in the research oriented observation the issues to be observed depend on the researcher's *problem* of interest and the *purpose* to be accomplished in regard to that problem. Two researchers, a theologian and a sociologist, can observe what is going on in a church setting in a very different way with respect to the research question each of them constructs and the purpose each of them wishes to accomplish. While the theologian may be interested in the way people worship God in that church setting,

45. Merriam, *Qualitative Research*, 94–95.

46. Kumar, *Research Methodology*, 119.

47. Merriam, *Qualitative Research*, 94.

48. Ibid., 96.

49. Ibid.

the sociologist may be interested in the way people interact among themselves. Obviously, the two researchers will construct two different research questions and will have two different purposes for their observational researches. This tells us that the researcher and his/her research problem and purpose are the determinants of what to be conceived in the research field.

However, due to human inability to observe everything happening in his/her surroundings as he/she begins the research, Merriam[50] lists some aspects that can be eye-breakers in the researcher's observational process. We quote these aspects at length including their subsequent questions:

1. *The physical setting*: What is the physical environment like? What is the context? What kind of behavior is the setting designed for? How is space allocated? What objects, resources, technologies are in the setting? The principal's office, the school bus, the cafeteria, and the classroom vary in physical attributes as well as in anticipated behavior.

2. *The participants*: Describe who is in the scene, how many people, and their roles. What brings these people together? Who is allowed here? Who is here who would be expected to be here? What are the relevant characteristics of the participants?

3. *Activities and interactions*: What is going on? Is there a definable sequence of activities? How are people and activities 'connected or interrelated-either from the participants' point of view or from the researcher's point of view (. . .). What norms or rules structure the activities and interactions? When did the activity begin? How long does it last? Is it a typical activity, or unusual?

4. *Conversation*: What is the content of conversations in this setting? Who speaks to whom? Who listens? Quote directly, paraphrase and summarize conversations. If possible, use a tape recorder to back up your note taking. Note silences and nonverbal behavior that add meaning to the exchange.

5. *Subtal factors*: Less but as important to observe are

   • Informal and unplanned activities

   • Symbolic and connotative meanings of words

   • Unobtrusive measures such as physical clues

50. Ibid., 97–98.

- 'What does *not* happen'—especially if it ought to happen (. . .)

6. *Your own behavior*: You are as much a part of the scene as participants. How is your role, whether as an observer or an intimate participant, affecting the scene you are observing? What do you say and do? In addition, what thoughts are you having about what is going on? These become 'observer comments,' an important part of field notes.[51]

In order to accomplish the above tasks in the observation process, the skills of the observer are needed. The observer must train oneself to be a skilled observer. "Training [oneself] to be a skilled observer includes 'learning how to write descriptively; practicing the disciplined recording of field notes; knowing how to separate detail from trivia . . . and using rigorous methods to validate observations' (. . .)."[52]

Despite the skills the researcher needs to have in order to carry out his/her observational research, he/she also needs to know how to enter the field, to collect the data and exit the field. The researcher must expect to handle the various questions and expectations of his/her group. Bogdam and Biklen list some of the questions that the researcher should expect to answer from the group of people he/she enters in order to observe: "What are you actually going to do? Will you be disruptive? What are you going to do with your findings? Why us? What will we get out of this?"[53]

After entry, the researcher will need to convince his/her participants to *accept* and *trust* him/her. This is the most important part the researcher can do in order to observe what is really going on. In order to do this, "the researcher [needs to] establish rapport by fitting into the participants' routine, finding some common ground with them, helping out on occasion, being friendly and showing interest in the activity."[54] Failure to establish rapport may lead to participants' hiding the real nature of the activity, and even avoiding the researcher. After gaining rapport the researcher needs to carry out an intensive collection of data. He/she has "to observe intently, remember as much as possible, and then record in as much detail as possible what has been observed."[55]

51. Merriam, *Qualitative Research*, 97–98.

52. Ibid, 95.

53. Bogdam & Biklen in Merriam, *Qualitative Research*, 99.

54. Ibid., 99.

55. Ibid., 99–100.

As the researcher immerses in the life of the informants, there is a point he/she will become part of the life of that group. At this point, leaving the group becomes difficult to the researcher because in so doing participants may feel offended by the researcher. The researcher can minimize this feeling by reducing the number of visits he/she makes to the group in order to observe as the day to leave approaches. The reduction of days to attend to the group will imply that the research is going to an end.[56]

Recording Observational Data

Kumar distinguishes four strategies for recording observational data: narrative, scales, categorical and recording in mechanical devices.[57] In *narrative recording*, the observer uses his/her own words to describe what he/she sees in the interaction. What he/she does is to make brief notes while observing that, that will make him/her remember while making extended descriptions afterwards. Narrative description can make the researcher provide a richer description of the interaction. At the same time, it is advantageous because the researcher can narrate his/her biases in the observation and description that can lead to biasness in his interpretations and conclusions. Forgetting to record an observation and incomplete recording are some other possibilities that can occur, hence causing unreliable narrative, interpretation and conclusions made.

In using scales to record data, the researcher establishes a scale in order to describe behavior. The *aspects of interaction* that the researcher observes are rated in a scale as positive, neutral or negative. The aspects of behavior in the group include: silence, rapport, eloquence, friendliness, etc.[58]

Categorical recording refers to the use of categories available in the interaction: "For example: passive/active (two categories); introvert/extrovert (two categories); strongly agree/agree/uncertain/disagree/strongly disagree (five categories).

Mechanical devices include videotapes or sound tape recorders. Videotaping the interaction enables the researcher to re-see it any time he/she wishes to describe the situation. In that case, it becomes more helpful as the actual interaction becomes visible when the researcher interprets and draws some conclusions from the observation. However, most people

56. Ibid., 100.

57. Kumar, *Research Methodology*, 121–22.

58. See diagram in Kumar, *Research Methodology*, 122.

change their behavior when they learn that they are being videotaped. This may hinder having the actual behavior of the group.

Types of Observations

Kumar distinguishes two types of observations: *participant* and *Non-participant* observations. In *participant observation* the researcher establishes a relationship with those he/she researches, stays with them in their own locations, participates fully in the activities, ceremonies, and rituals of the group being observed. The participant observer strives to learn the code of life of the people being observed in order to understand the meaning of what they say and do.

The researcher may want to observe the reaction of the community towards street children. In order to do this the researcher has to act or participate in most activities of the street children. This participation will enable the researcher to know the real situation that street children face. The researcher may want to investigate the attitude of church members towards drunkard people during church services, the researcher will have to drink or just participate in the activities of drunkard people during church services. This will help him/her know the reality about the relationship between drunkard people and other members of the church during church worship services.

This group being observed can either know or not know that they are being observed for research purpose. Wilson categorizes participant observation as being disguised or covert and undisguised participant observations. In disguised participant observation the subjects are unaware that they are being observed for research purposes. One advantage of this category is that subjects may not change the behavior in the presence of the researcher, and therefore enable the observer to obtain the real data he/she longed for. The disadvantage of course is that this type of observation breaks ethical obligations of informed consent.

The second category is undisguised participant observation whereby the researcher tells subjects straight away the purpose of his/her research and his observation. The disadvantage is obvious. Subjects may change their behavior in the presence of the observer. Hence they may render the researcher obtain inadequate or unwanted data. The advantage is that it follows all ethical obligations regarding the freedom of the participant in the research process.[59]

59. Wilson, *Essentials of Business Research*, 159–60.

The *non-participant observation* takes place without the researcher being involved in the activities of those he/she observes. He/she remains a passive observer, just watching and listening to what is going on at a distance without directly interacting with those being observed. His/her main role is to just note or record whatever he/she observes without influencing their behavior. For example, the researcher may want to observe and report about what is going on at football games between the followers of the two playing teams. What he/she will have to do is just enter the playground, observe what is going on at a distance and record it for future analysis. The researcher can be interested in knowing the relationship between pastors and people during burial services, the relationship between teachers and students in class and out of class, the relationship between children and parents in homes, the behavior of Christians away from their pastors, the behavior of bishops when they meet together as a group, etc. In all these activities, and others left unmentioned, the researcher can just be a passive observer and listener of what is going on. His role is to carefully record the interactions for further analysis.[60]

Some Disadvantages of Observation

There are many disadvantages of using observation as a method for collecting field research data. Kumar lists four of these disadvantages:

> When individuals or groups become aware that they are being observed, they may change their behaviour. (. . .). When a change in behaviour of a person or groups is attributed to their being observed it is known as the Howthorne Effect. The use of observation in such a situation may introduces [sic!] distortion: what is observed may not represent their normal behaviour. There is always the possibility of observer bias. If the observer is biased, s/he can easily introduce bias and there is no easy way to verify the observation and the inferences drawn from them. The interpretations drawn from observations may vary from observer to observer. There is the possibility of incomplete observation and / or recording, which varies with method of recording (. . .).[61]

Hence, the disadvantages listed above indicate that observation as a research method cannot avoid running the risk of producing data that are

60. Kumar, *Research Methodology*, 120.

61. Ibid.

likely to be unreliable. However the reliability or unreliability of data produced will depend on the context of the research and the approach of the researcher as an observer.

Conclusion

Without research, you have no right to speak. Why? This is because you do not have any evidence to support what you speak. Research makes the acquisition of evidence possible. Evidence makes the researcher support his/her reasons for a particular stand point concerning the problem stated. In this case, the researcher needs to be sure that the evidence collected is strong and convincingly valuable to support what he/she asserts.

This chapter concerned about the way the researcher can collect the intended data as evidence for his/her argument. This chapter has argued that the way the researcher selects the instrument for data collection, and the way the researcher uses that instrument for this purpose, matters a lot in obtaining reliable data to answer his/her research question. The chapter has emphasized that despite the various instruments that can be used, the researcher and his/her ability to perceive the field is the primary instrument for data collection. In this case, the chapter is important for researchers because it shows that the type of data to be collected depend mainly on the type of instrument which the researcher decides to use.

Chapter Highlight

1. Data is any material or information collected from the source for a purpose of answering a research question.

2. The way the researcher selects the instrument for data collection, and the way the researcher uses that instrument in the data collection matters a lot in obtaining reliable data.

3. The researcher himself/herself is the primary instrument for field data collection. Other instruments include interviews, and observations.

Study Questions

1. Discuss the differences between primary and secondary data and the way each type of data is collected.

2. Using as many other literatures as possible, discuss the two main instruments of collecting qualitative field research data: interviews and observation.

3. What does it mean to say that the researcher is the primary instrument in the process of data collection?

10

Arguing Your Case

"Writing requires the creation of a series of drafts until the final composition emerges. Many years a go, a close friend of ours (. . .) casually reflected on his writing: 'Writing is a lot like having a baby. You go through months of pregnancy. The baby grows. You experience frustrations and elation, depression and expectation. There is labor. You work hard. The baby is born. I feel like I am pregnant when I write.' Writing is the conception, gestation, and maturation of an idea."

—MACHI & MCEVOY, *THE LITERATURE REVIEW*, 142.

Introduction

AFTER THE RESEARCHER HAS collected the materials (evidence) on the problem of his/her research using the instruments discussed above, adhering to all the ethical issues involved in the data collection process discussed above, analyzed the data collected and interpreted them to hear what they mean, now he/she needs to use this material to support his/her assumptions/propositions. The researcher has to argue a case. This is because the goal of research is not only to discover issues, or phenomena about the research question, but also to communicate that discovery to other people in the community. By 'community' here we mean other researchers, government authorities, informants, or any other general public that may benefit from the conducted research. This means that the research carried out should have an intended audience and that audience should be able to learn something potential from this research. If the research carried out will not be understood by the intended audience, it will be considered to have failed to fulfill the promised goals stated in the beginning of inquiry.[1]

Therefore, in this chapter we present the way in which the researcher can argue his/her case in order to communicate the research findings clearly and convincingly. We begin with an elaboration of what arguing a case really means, shows how the research report presents a specific case, analyse the things to consider in producing a well-presented research report as a case, and present the contents of a well-presented and well-argued research report. This chapter indicates an important final attempt of the researcher to write his first draft in order to understand more clearly the results of his/her research, and the revisions of this draft in order to make it readable and understandable to his/her readers..

What does It Mean by 'Arguing a Case?'

The researcher does the communication highlighted above through arguing his/her case. In arguing a case, the researcher needs to construct a coherent, clear, logical and persuasive argument to support his/her proposition. This means that writing a scholarly essay is always developing and defending ones ideas using the evidence gathered in the research process. Ideas defended can be many, but only one idea is the heart of the whole research essay. This is the main idea which all other small ideas will point to in the writing process. This means that when the researcher presents his/her research report, he/she defends the individual ideas which eventually lead to the defense of the main idea of the report. The main idea or small ideas presented are defended by the provision of *reasons* that explain why readers should believe that your main idea in the research is valid. The main idea which the researcher defends is called a *claim*. Hence, the whole process of putting forward a claim, providing strong reasons to the claim as to why readers should believe in your main idea followed by reliable evidence to support your reasons is called *arguing a case*, or *developing an informed argument*.

Claims to be defended are stated in different ways. A claim can be in a statement form or in a question form. If stated in a statement form a claim

1. Chambliss & Schutt, *Making Sense*, 273.

requires to be followed by reasons which are in turn backed up by reliable evidence that will persuade readers to believe in the validity of the main idea proposed. If stated in a question form, the claim will require answers (reasons) that are backed up by evidence to persuade readers to believe that the answers provided respond to the posed question. Let us now look at the examples of the two types of claims below:

Statement Form: *Pastors Are Rich People in Our Society.*

This is a direct claim that needs reasons to justify why one thinks that pastors are rich people. It also needs some evidence to justify the provided reasons.

Question Form: *Why are Pastors Rich People in Our Society?*

This is an indirect claim. It is not different from the above claim. To ask "why pastors are rich people in our society" is to have in mind that pastors are rich people; and so it needs some reasons in order to justify their richness to you. In both cases you need some reasons and evidence to persuade readers to believe that pastors are rich people in your society. In this case, arguing a case or developing an argument is providing strong reasons and concrete evidence to support a particular statement or claim or answering a particular question.

What are the characteristics of a good evidence to support a particular claim or answer a particular question? This question is important to note because not all evidence is adequate to support the provided reasons for a particular claim. Judith Ferster provides us four characteristics of good evidence: first, it should be *sufficient*. This means that it needs to have as enough data as possible to try to convince the reader about the reasons for the provided claim. Second, the evidence needs to be *typical*. This means that the provided evidence has to have enough representation of what is purported in the claim and reasons of the argument. Third, the evidence has to be *accurate*. This accuracy of the evidence will be vivid in the correctness it portrays to the reader's judgment, and fourth, the evidence has to fit the claim. This means that it has to be *relevant* to what is claimed and to the provided reasons. Therefore, the four characteristics: sufficiency, typicality, accuracy, and relevance are important to qualify the sound evidence of reasons provided to support a particular claim.[2]

Stating the claim in the form of a question is common in most research reports. Researchers wonder about a particular phenomenon occurring in the society and raise a question (or questions) about it. The question raised is the starting point for research. The purpose of research is searching for answers (reasons and evidence) to that question. In this case, the formulation of the question that the researcher does, the answers (reasons and evidence) that the researcher provides to the question and any other explanations that the researcher provides to justify that the answer provided is satisfactory is actually what is called a scientific research report (or a research argument).

The above explanation of a case assumes that the researcher takes a certain stand in his/her claim. However, it is possible to defend a claim without taking any particular side. The researcher can explore a phenomenon appearing in his/her society for the sake of making it open or making it clear for other researchers. This is also a legitimate way of approaching at research issues. The main problem with this way is that it hardly makes an argument that is simple for the reader to follow, especially in knowing the researcher's own stand. Readers can easily think that the researcher is uncertain with what he/she is claiming. In whatever way of arguing a case, the most important thing is to remember that academic reporting or arguing about a particular case is providing reasons and evidence for what one is trying to say (to claim).

If one has to develop a clear, logical, coherent and persuasive argument in presenting his/her research report, then what is an argument, and why is it so important in research? According to Hart, "An argument involves putting forward reasons to influence someone's belief that what you are proposing is the case (. . .). Whichever way someone makes an argument they are attempting to convince others of the validity (or logic) of how they see the world and convince us that we should see it the way they do."[3]

Arguments are important in research because they help researchers to explore the world by exploring the nature of reality (ontology) in their fields of study and finding new ways to understand that reality (epistemology). In doing that, valid knew knowledge is generated through evaluating

2. Ferster, *Arguing through Literature*, 152.

3. Hart, *Doing Literature Review*, 80.

previous arguments about existing concepts, topics, standpoints, or existing knowledge about a phenomenon.[4]

What Are the Major Components of an Argument?

According to Hart, an argument has two main components that make it plausible: 'a point one makes' and 'a reason for that point'. This means that in order to construct a sound argument one needs to "make a point (or statement)" by "providing sufficient reason for the point to be accepted by others."[5] The sequence does not matter. One can provide the reasons and then make a point based on the reasons, or make a point and then provide reasons for that point. The argument formation can be either way, but the purpose of the argument remains the same: to make a claim that is supported by reasons and evidence, which is a valid argument. The argument has a good structure of its formulation. Remember, we are not saying that such kind of argument is a 'sound' argument, because for an argument to be 'sound' it must have true premises or propositions.

Arguments are made up of propositions. A proposition is a statement within an argument. It may be true or false. In this case propositions are statements in an argument that other people may agree or disagree. Look at the example below:

Teachers earn a lot of money in their teaching work (first premise).

I want to earn a lot of money myself (second premise).

Therefore I should become a teacher (conclusion).

The first two propositions above are called PREMISES. Premises are propositions of assumed fact, that are set in order to provide reasons and evidences for convincing other people to believe in one's claim, i.e. the conclusion. The third proposition in the above argument is the conclusion. The conclusion one makes is the claim of that argument.

For a simple argument, it is possible to have few premises and a conclusion to sum up the argument. But in most cases arguments have *Inferences*. Inferences are the reasoning part of the argument. Look at the example below:

- *Pastors earn a lot of money from their work* (a premise).

4. Ibid., 81.
5. Ibid., 80.

- *With a lot of money, a person can buy many expensive clothes* (a premise).

- *Pastors buy a lot of expensive clothes* (inference or inferential claim from premises 1 and 2).

- *Therefore, I should become a pastor* (factual claim from 3 and 4).

How should the researcher organize his/her argument? In logic, there are two lines of arguing one can follow in presenting his/her argument: deductive and inductive arguments. What are deductive and inductive arguments? We discussed these terms in a more detail in chapter two above. But for the purpose of the way the researcher needs to organize his argument, we will repeat a little beat more here. Hart provides the following definitions for these terms: Deduction, on the one hand, "is commonly a statement or theory whose truth or falsity is known in advance of experience or observation (a priori: prior to experience)—referring to instances of reasoning in which the conclusion follows from the premises. Deduction (or inference) can proceed from the general to particular, general to general and particular to particular."[6]

Induction, on the other hand, "is commonly a statement whose truth or falsity is made more probable by the accumulation of confirming evidence (a posteriori: based on experience)—referring to instances of reasoning in which statements are made about a phenomenon based on observations of instances of that phenomenon. It consists in arguing that because all instances of a so far observed have the property b, all further observations of a will also have property b."[7] As we stated above, most field researches aim at accumulating evidence in order to provide expressions to existing situation. This means that the expression of the existing situation depends sorely on the data collected. Therefore induction is the frequently used organization of presenting research findings in field researches.

Research Report as an Argued Case

A well presented, well-documented and well-argued case is called a *Research Report*. A successfully presented case must have a convincing organization and written clearly for the reader to understand. As a case, the research report

6. Ibid., 82.
7. Ibid (emphasis is mine).

is clear, concise, readable, and logical. This means that it follows the principles of logic to form a coherent argument. The report is not arguments; it is only one main argument which is formed by small arguments in it, and which in turn all support the main argument of the whole research report. The small arguments have premises, evidences and conclusions, and so is the main argument of the whole research report. Therefore, the coherence of the whole research report and its logical organization are the ones that make this research to be clear, concise, understandable, and meaningful.

How will the researcher present his research findings argumentatively and with a coherent logical organization? In fact presenting the research report in an argumentative way, with a persuasive organization needs time and commitment to the research work already done. Nancy Jean Vyhmeister rightly notes: "Excellent [research report] writing takes time and effort. Mediocre writing is faster and easier. However, it does not usually merit the professor's approval, reader's interest, or [the researcher's] own satisfaction."[8]

As we said above, mere doing of research is not enough to accomplish the research process. Ndunguru states this point clearly when he writes: "in a communication encounter, nothing has been communicated unless the message is encoded, sent, received, and understood by the recipient."[9] The researcher needs to be committed to presenting what has been obtained from research in a way that will be understandable to the intended audience. Chambliss and Schutt also outline several principles to bear in mind in the process of writing a well-presented, well-argued, and well-documented research report.[10] We describe these principles below.

First, as a researcher, you should pay respect to "the complexity of the task and don't expect to write a polished draft in a linear fashion. Your thinking will develop as you write, causing you to reorganize and rewrite."[11] This means that writing an effective, convincing and well-polished research report is impossible when the researcher obtains the first draft of his/her report. The researcher does not need to be satisfied by the good English he/she uses, good sentences, or good material organizations in the produced first draft. This is because the process from the beginning of writing to producing the first draft is writing for the researcher *to understand* his/her research product. This

---

8. Vyhmeister, *Quality Research Papers*, 115.

9. Ndunguru, *Lectures on Research*, 135.

10. Chamblis & Schutt, *Making Sense*, 273–74.

11. Ibid., 273.

draft is the preliminary step towards the real report whereby the researcher writes in order to *be understood* by his/her readers.[12]

Machi and McEvoy note clearly about writing to understand and writing to be understood: "Writing [to understand and be understood] requires the creation of a series of drafts until the final composition emerges. Many years a go, a close friend of ours (. . .) casually reflected on his writing: 'Writing is a lot like having a baby. You go through months of pregnancy. The baby grows. You experience frustrations and elation, depression and expectation. There is labor. You work hard. The baby is born. I feel like I am pregnant when I write.'"[13] This means that you will have to audit and edit your work in writing as many drafts as possible towards the final one: audit and edit the content to ensure the consistency of ideas, audit and edit the grammar to correct all misused words and phrases, ensure good use of punctuations and spellings, continuity of persons, the use of mostly active voice in the document, and the use of suitable transitions between one chapter and another and one paragraph to another.

Chambliss and Schutt write thus about reviewing and writing drafts: "As you review the first draft, you will see many ways to improve your writing."[14] Since it is, in most cases, easier to add materials to the first draft than to remove what has already been written, Chambliss and Schutt emphasize that the researcher should "Focus particularly on how to shorten and clarify (. . .) statements." The researcher has to "Make sure that each paragraph concerns only one topic."[15] Therefore the researcher needs to think more about the report after producing the first draft of it in order to suit the understanding of the intended audience.

Second, as a researcher, you should "Leave enough time for dead ends, restarts, revisions, and so on, and accept the fact that you will discard much of what you write."[16] This means that writing a well organized and meaningful research report needs a disciplined time management. Time management is essential because the end times of writing are always hectic, frustrating and disturbing. Revisions, omissions and rectifications of the report are important events at the end times.

12. Cf. Machi & McEvoy, *The Literature Review*, 129–52.

13. Machi & McEvoy, *The Literature Review*, 142.

14. Chamblis & Schutt, *Making Sense*, 274.

15. Ibid.

16. Ibid., 273.

However, these events demand the researcher to devote enough time for dealing with them. If time is not enough, it is possible to distort even the work which the researcher has already done. This will happen because he/she will discard some important materials because of hectic situation faced by the researcher. Therefore the important thing is that the researcher needs to be flexible with what he/she has written. The researcher needs to accept the reality that what is written is just a proposal that is subject to modifications towards the better one. These modifications need a devotion of enough time that will enable the researcher to deal with them in an efficient way.

Theorists of research Barry H. Kantowitz, Henry L. Roediger III and David G. Elmes advise us that *"good writing requires good editing.* Never submit your first draft of a research paper. (. . .). Revise your report as many times as are necessary to make it clear. A successful research report requires several drafts before it is done. Also remember that writing usually takes longer than you anticipate. Allow yourself time to do the job."[17]

The above piece of advice is essential to all researchers, whether amateur or experienced, because the first draft is always a preliminary work the researcher has done. It is not a completed work. The first draft is the beginning of more thinking and writing. More work is to be done to the draft in order to do justice to the presented findings and conclusions. This is mostly what it means when we say that the researcher should neither try to write a polished first draft not be satisfied that the produced first draft is satisfactory. This is because as the researcher or other readers of the draft read and re-read it, they will discover a considerable number of important issues which need revisions.

Third, as a researcher, you need to "write as fast as you can. Don't worry about spelling, grammar, and so on until you are polishing things up."[18] This statement elaborates the above point of time management. Time management goes together with the knowledge of the researcher's work and the plan to complete it. In order for the researcher to complete his/her work in the required time, he/she has to write with a considerable speed in order to finish the first draft. It is always better to work on the manuscript at hand rather than constructing a new manuscript. Therefore, the researcher does not need to care much about spellings, grammar and other trivial things

---

17. Kantowitz, Roediger III & David G. Elmes, *Experimental Psychology*, 110 (emphasis is in original).

18. Chamblis & Schutt, *Making Sense*, 273.

while struggling to produce the first draft because these will be taken care of during the polishing stage of his writing process.

Fourth, as a researcher, you should "Ask any one you trust for their reaction to what you have written."[19] This statement means that writing of the research report is the work of the researcher, but polishing it is the work of any one with good wills. Bryman says that in your writing process "Try to get as much feedback on your writing as possible and respond positively to the points anyone makes about what they read. (. . .). Their comments may be very useful, by and large, your supervisor's comments are the main ones you should seek."[20] Robert W. Pazmiño provides a similar advice when he states: "The process of refining work requires perseverance and a willingness to receive constructive feedback from others. Developing habits of reviewing work and allowing others to respond can greatly improve the quality of work (. . .)."[21]

Bryman's statement above indicates that there is no need for the research to depend on the researcher's mind alone as being the all-knowing. There are other people like: friends, classmates, supervisors, fellow researchers, fellow department members and so on who can be potential sources for ideas to nourish the written report. There is no use for the researcher to try eating an elephant for himself/herself and end up in frustrations and producing an academically unsatisfactory research report! Pazmiño rightly advises: "Our writing requires the eyes of and thoughts of others to improve and to effectively communicate beyond our personal sphere."[22] Therefore, as also Chambliss and Schutt warn, you should "Seek criticism from friends, teachers, or other research consumers before you turn in the final product. They will alert you to problems in the research or the writing."[23]

The above-mentioned people will help the researcher to polish his/her report making it more readable and persuasive. Bryman notes that being persuasive "means that you must convince your readers of the credibility of your conclusions. (. . .). You must persuade your readers that your findings and conclusions are significant and that they are plausible."[24] Therefore

---

19. Ibid., 274.

20. Bryman, *Social Science Research*, 530.

21. Pazmiño, *Doing Theological Research*, 10.

22. Ibid., 45.

23. Chamblis & Schutt, *Making Sense*, 274.

24. Bryman, *Social Science Research*, 530.

other readers may be helpful to the researcher to ascertain the way the report can be persuasive through their suggestions and inputs.

Fifth, as a researcher, you should "Write as you go along, so you have notes and report segments drafted even before you focus on writing the report."[25] This means that you have to start your writing earlier. Bryman suggests one important reason for starting to write the research report earlier: to avoid the tendency of "writing being left until the last minute and consequently rushed."[26] Bryman advises researcher that since presenting the report findings and conclusions are important stages in the research process, the researcher needs to start earlier in writing his/her report in order to provide a convincing account of such aspects.

The researcher always needs to know that writing is always a process. It goes with thinking and evaluating what one thinks and puts on paper. In a qualitative field research, the researcher needs to do the analysis and interpretation of data along with his data collection process. In doing this analysis and interpretation the researcher will have to write some segments of what he/she understands from the themes and categories arising from the analysis. This is what it really means by starting to write the research report earlier.

The produced segments can be of great help in the report writing process because they will reduce the task of the researcher. Instead of thinking anew from the bulk of the collected data, the researcher will use the written notes of the analyzed and interpreted evidence to support his/her argument for the case being argued. These notes will be a starting point for the writing process. The researcher will acquire new ideas to polish and focus the report as he/she continues with the process of writing. Therefore the written notes will also be important in helping the researcher to make a focus on what was researched, what needs to be reported to the intended audience, and in preparing the tentative outline for the report.

A Well-Presented Field Research Report

The question here is on the way to begin writing a well-presented report. How should the researcher begin writing his research report document? There is no clearly known formula on the way to start. Some people prefer to start with the writing of an introduction, while others start with some sort of tentative outline to guide them on the way. In whatever the case, "In

25. Chamblis & Schutt, *Making Sense*, 274.
26. Bryman, *Social Science Research*, 529.

scientific writing, you write for two specific goals: to inform readers and to persuade readers."[27] These two goals are worth taking into account when the researcher begins to write his/her research report.

Michael Alley emphasizes that in order for the researcher to write a well-presented scientific report document, the researcher has to consider four important aspects. Alley writes thus: "In scientific writing, there are four principal constraints to consider: the audience for the document, the *format* for the document, the mechanics of the document, and the politics surrounding the document."[28] We will briefly discuss these aspects below.

Consider the Audience

John M. Swales and Christine B. Feak in their book *Academic Writing for Graduate Students* warn researchers about the importance of the audience of the report. They write: "To be successful in your writing task, you need to have an understanding of your audience's expectations and prior knowledge, because these will affect the content of your writing."[29] The audience here means the readers of the research report document. Readers of the document determine the way the researcher should present his/her document. The researcher may aim his research document to be read by none academicians, or by academicians. The researcher may aim at a particular group of people, such as teachers, pastors, accountants, etc., as readers; or the researcher can aim at all groups of people. In whatever the case, the researcher's decision about the type of audience is the main determinant of the language and vocabulary to be used in the presentation of his/her research report.

The language and vocabulary used by the researcher for academicians cannot be used for none academicians and vice versa. This means that the researcher needs to avoid pedantic writing as much as possible. "Pedantic writing," Rubin and Rubin write, "uses too many big words, too many abstract ideas and phrases, and to many references to the literature."[30] This way of writing bores the reader and makes the report unreadable. Rubin and Rubin advise the field researcher: "Whenever possible use ordinary words, not special technical ones. If you use a technical word, make sure

27. Alley, *The Craft of Scientific Writing*, 3.

28. Ibid.

29. Swales & Feak, *Academic Writing*, 8.

30. Rubin & Rubin, *Qualitative Interviewing*, 268.

it is defined the first time you use it. Eliminate long, complex sentences."[31] Hence, the above words of Rubin and Rubin indicate that the writing of research report needs to be audience sensitive, or in other words contextual.

Michael Alley further warns field researchers that "No matter what [field research] document you are writing, you should assess the audience: (1) who will read the document, (2) what do they know about the subject, (3) why will they read the document, and (4) how will they read the document. These questions dictate how you write the document."[32] Therefore, the above issues compel the researcher to consider the type of target people for his/her research report, their knowledge of the subject which he/she communicates to them, and which will help him/her to define or not define some of the used terms.

When the researcher has a mixture of people to whom the report is targeted, he/she is under obligation to consider the primary thought audience first then the secondary audience. The primary audience needs to dominate the writing mind of the researcher over the secondary. This means that it is hardly possible to write the report which fully satisfies all audiences purported by the researcher.[33]

The issues above compel the researcher to consider the type of information his/her audience would need to get from the researcher in the field research document. It is obvious that not all research materials will need to be reported in the research report; only the important materials will be reported. For example, in the report written for academicians as target audience the researcher will have to present materials according to the needs of academicians, for the sake of them and in the way which academicians can understand.[34]

The issues above further compel researchers to consider the behavior of most audiences. Some audiences can hardly read the whole report. They may be interested in only a few parts of the research report. The field researcher has to be considerate of this behavior when writing his/her report. Through considering the behavior of the audience the field researcher can discern some places of the report which he/she will need to put much emphasis and where he/she will need to leave without emphasis.[35] Therefore the above

31. Ibid.
32. Alley, *The Craft of Scientific Writing*, 5.
33. Ibid., 5–6.
34. Ibid., 6.
35. Ibid.

expressions of audience indicate that extra attention towards this aspect is needed when the researcher considers a well-presented field research report.

Consider the Format Required for Your Report

Alley defines the format of the field research document as being "the way in which a document or presentation is arranged. Format includes such things as the choice of typeface, the spacing between sections, [and] the referencing system for sources."[36] The crucial thing to take into account here is that there is no single format which is universal for all research reports in the world. Formats are contextually based; they are localized to institutions, or journals which enforce research to be done. Therefore, the researcher is obliged to follow the format of the institution he/she belongs or the journal he/she is interested to publish the field research report.[37]

Consider the Mechanics of the Report

Mechanics refers to issues like grammar, spelling and punctuations. These issues may seem to be trivial to the field researcher because he/she is mainly concerned about ideas and arguments. However, they are very important issues if such ideas and arguments are to be understood at all. The researcher needs to mind the grammatical constructions needed for the researcher to produce a document which readers will appreciate as being written professionally and thoughtfully. The researcher needs to do two things: editing and proofreading. He/she needs to check the grammatical constructions of the report to suite the logic of the argument. He/she also needs to check the spellings and punctuation marks. In doing this the researcher will make the report readable.

Consider the Politics Surrounding Your Report Writing

By the politics surrounding the report we mean the way in which the field researcher needs to be honest to what has been obtained from the research process. Any report depends sorely on the honesty of the researcher in presenting the results of the research. The readers of the report were not

36. Ibid., 274.
37. Ibid., 7.

there when the research was conducted and neither do they know what happened and what was collected. Despite convincing the reader to believe what is presented, the researcher needs to present the findings honestly and with good will to further knowledge. Therefore, honesty to what was obtained from field research process surrounds the politics of the report which the researcher has to present to readers.

What Constitutes a Good Field Research Report?

The discussion in the section above centered on the four aspects to consider in writing a well-presented field research report. However, the Questions are: what makes a good field research report? How can the researcher know that he/she has produced an excellently convincing field research report? The simple answer to the second question is that the researcher in a college or university will know when the marks have been awarded for the report. In a funding urgency the researcher will know when the report has been accepted for funding! In a journal, the researcher will know when his/her article will be accepted for publication.

However, it is important to respond to the first question: what constitutes a good field research report? The following are some of the important features that constitute a good field research report: foundations, research design, argument, and coherence. We briefly discuss each of these aspects below.

Foundations of the Research

The researcher should bear in mind that a good research report must be located within a large field of knowledge. It cannot come from the air. It identifies its place in it and contributes to knowledge within that area. This is the foundation of the field research and is attained through a thorough and thoughtful review of previous researches about the researcher's study problem. Through the review of the existing knowledge within that area, the report will identify the gap in the existing scholarship and the importance of the research will be shown on the way it tries to deal with that gap. The researcher needs to tell in the introductory part of the report what readers should expect in the researcher's endeavor to deal with the identified gap of knowledge. Therefore it is important that research is built upon the concrete and highly commendable existing knowledge and tries its best to contribute to that knowledge through identifying the gap and then try-ing to bridge it.

Research Design Used

The researcher cannot perform any field research without designing the way he/she will execute it. We have discussed research designs in the previous chapters; but, it is better we further emphasize here that a good research report depends on the way the researcher executed the research, and the good research depends mainly on the way in which the researcher designed the research itself. The researcher needs to state more clearly all method-ological issues in such a way that they indicate that they can be replicated. The approach to research should show that the researcher is knowledgeable and knows well what he/she is doing. Moreover, using the chosen design, the researcher should present his/her results quite well, with an appropri-ate design of presentation. The researcher needs also to show that he/she has labored at interpreting the results obtained with an adequate mean of interpretation.

Well-Presented and Well-Documented Argument

This chapter is concerned about arguing your case. We have discussed above what an argument is and the way the researcher should present his/her argument. In this part we just explain, with more emphasis, what is required of a good research report? We want to emphasize that a good research report has a well-structured and well-focused argument. The vari-ous links of the argument must be shown and explained clearly. Therefore, the way the researcher structures his/her argument in terms of chapters and subchapters, and the way such structure enhances the persuasive presenta-tion of the argument are essential for a good report.

The good presentation alone is not enough to make an argument per-suasive. The argument must show clearly the claims made by the researcher, the reasons for the claims, and the evidence for the provided reasons. The evidence should come from strong and reliable sources. In field research report, we expect the researcher to document both primary and secondary data. The well-documented argument is attractive to read and persuades the reader to believe what has been reported. Moreover, the researcher should follow a recognized referencing system in the discipline which the researcher belongs and he/she should be consistent with that system.

In this case, though we do not use such a style in this book, we still recommend Turabian Kate L. (2007) *A handbook of writers of term papers, theses, and dissertations* (7th Edition). Revised by Wayn C. Booth, Gregory G. Colomb, Joseph M. Williams, and The University of Chicago Press Editorial Staff. Chicago: The University of Chicago Press. This book reflects *The Chicago manual of style* (2003) (15th Edition). Chicago: The University Press, authored by the University of Chicago. These referencing systems are widely used in various levels of advanced research.

The field researcher should know that the report presents only one argument. However, as we discussed above in this chapter, the field researcher should know that this argument is made up of smaller arguments in various sections, all with the aim of supporting the main argument. With this knowledge, the researcher has to make a balance of what he/she presents in the argument. The various sections in the argument, and what they constitute, should be in line with what is purported by the main argument. In this case, the balance between the chapters and sub-chapters as smaller arguments should maintain the coherence of the argument and should aim at making the logical presentation of the whole report.

The attention should be paid in the writing of chapters and paragraphs within the report. Each chapter should present one main idea and that idea should be related to the idea of the whole report. Nancy Jean Vyhmeister emphasizes that every chapter within the report "must be a self-contained unit. That is, everything on one topic should be in the same chapter. Everything in one section should be related to the same matter; no extraneous material should be allowed."[38] This means that the researcher should create a good link between one chapter and the other in order to make a good flow of the argument.

Even paragraphs needs to be well-written with remarkable unity and coherence. This means that the paragraph has to have only one unifying thought and every sentence in the paragraph contributes to that thought. Each paragraph needs to have a topic sentence that carries the idea of the paragraph and every sentence in the paragraph should support that idea. Paragraphs and chapters should be linked together by transition words. Moreover, there should be a remarkable relationship between one sentence and the other from the topic sentence in the first line of the paragraph to the

38. Vyhmeister, *Quality Research Papers*, 107.

concluding sentence. Therefore, this logical flow of sentences, paragraphs, and chapters will make the report convincing and admirable to read.

The coherence and unity of paragraphs, chapters and eventually the whole report depends very much on the use of what we call 'transitional words or phrases' and the proper introductions to quoted words. Transitional words or phrases make a link between one idea and another or help the field researcher move from one idea to another. Some of the words used to make a transition are the following: therefore, moreover, similarly, also, however, in conclusion, hence, meanwhile, in addition, eventually, finally, thus, consequently, also, likewise, first, second, third, . . . etc. These types of words are common in academic writing and make paragraphs and chapters more organized and smooth to read. However, the field researcher needs to understand the meaning of the word and an appropriate place to use it.[39]

When writing the report, the researcher will have to quote words of other people. There is a need for the field researcher to introduce the author or the speaker of the quoted words. It greatly displeases the reader to see the quotation just hanging into the page without knowing where it comes from, what is it all about; or it bothers the reader when he/she is obliged to look at the footnote down to discover who wrote it. The researcher needs to introduce the quotation within the text. In doing that the researcher needs to bear in mind the correct tense of when the event took place.

To refer to a past event the researcher needs to use past tense: Elima John noted . . . To refer to a present event, use present: Elima John notes . . . and for the future event use future tense: Elima John will note . . . It should be clear that the quotation words need to be preceded by a colon or comma. Therefore, words like: mentions, accepts, suggests, notes, reports, presupposes, believes, stipulates, agrees, declares, defends, states, affirms, describes, argues, adds, verifies, etc are commonly used by researchers to introduce quotations. However, the field researcher needs to understand well what the owner of the quotation does in that quotation and has to use an appropriate word in the quotation.[40]

The field researcher has to bear in mind that the presentation of the results in the argument is crucial. The field researcher should not present the field materials alone. As we said in the previous paragraphs in this sub-section, the field research report needs to use both primary and secondary data. The field researcher needs to discuss the results along with the existing

39. Ibid., 118.
40. Ibid., 119.

literature. He/she should show clearly within the discussion the convergence and divergence between what was obtained from field research and what exists in current literature. Hence, the field researcher needs to present the report in a full and convincing way. All conclusions made by the researcher from the discussion should be grounded upon data from both primary and secondary sources used and not on opinions or speculations of the researcher.

At the conclusion of his/her report the researcher is expected to do two things: first, to analyze the key results presented and discussed in the body of the report; and second, to provide a future perspective on the research work just done.[41] The researcher should briefly address his/her research objectives and the way these objectives relate to the outcome of the research. Does the outcome relate to the objectives that the researcher had; or does it differ from them? The field researcher needs to be clear on what should be done after his/her research by providing his/her suggestions and comments.

Conclusion

This chapter discussed about the responsibility of the field researcher to communicate his/her findings to readers. This is what arguing a case is all about. The chapter has discussed various ways through which the field researcher can argue his/her case. The chapter demonstrated that arguing a case is mainly playing with drafts of the report. The writing process from the beginning to the production of the first draft is for the sake of the researcher's own understanding, and the process of revising from the first draft to the final draft is for being understood by the readers. This chapter has therefore shown that writing research from the beginning to the end is a researcher's struggle, a frustrating but promising struggle.

The chapter has argued that the first draft of the report should not make the researcher satisfied. The researcher needs to audit and edit the report. In auditing the report the researcher needs to have enough time for this work. The researcher has to audit and edit the grammar, the words and phrases, flow of materials redundancies, transitions between paragraphs and chapters, and the general style of writing. In this case, the way to a convincing field research report is a hard way that needs courage and perseverance. It is like being pregnant, expecting for a baby to be born!

41. Alley, *The Craft of Scientific Writing*, 41.

Chapter Highlights

1. The purpose of writing a field research report is to communicate the research findings to respective readers.

2. The communication of findings to readers is done through arguing a case by the use of collected, analyzed, and interpreted field research data.

3. The report writing process produces an argued case. From the beginning of the writing process to the production of the first draft, the researcher writes for the sake of understanding himself/herself. Nevertheless, from the first draft to the final draft, the researcher writes for the sake of the readers' understanding.

4. Therefore, the researcher does not need to be satisfied by the production of the first draft. The first draft is just the beginning of writing for the researcher's readers of field report.

Study Questions

1. After the researcher has collected the data, analyzed and interpreted it, he/she has to 'argue a case.' What does it mean by '*arguing a case*'?

2. Outline the major components of an argument.

3. Why do we call the field research report 'an argued case'?

4. Discuss the main issues to consider when writing a well-presented research report.

5. Discuss the two main aspects that the researcher is expected to do when concluding the research report.

Bibliography

Alley, Michael. *The Craft of Scientific Writing*. Third Edition. Spring Street, New York: Springer Science Business Media, 1996.

Agar, Michael H. *The Professional Stranger: An Informal Introduction to Ethnography*. New York: Academic Press, 1980.

Ary, Donald, Jacobs, Lucy Cheser & Razavieh, Asghar. *Introduction to Research in Education*, Fifth Edition. Fort Worth, San Antonio: Harcourt Brace College, 1996.

Barbour, Rosaline. *Doing Focus Groups*. Los Angels: SAGE, 2007.

Barth, Fredrik, *Process and Form in social Life: Selected Essays of Fredrik Barth*, vol. I. London, Boston & Honley: Routledge & Kegan Paul, 1981.

Bein, Bernard C. & Bein, Agatha M. *Effective writing in Psychology: Papers, Posters, and Presentations*. Malden, Massachusetts: Blackwell, 2008.

Boyer, Ernest. *Scholarship Reconsidered: Priorities of the Professionate*. Princeton, New Jersey: Carnegie Foundation, 1990.

Brause, Rita S. *Writing Your Doctoral Dissertation: Invisible Rules for Success*. London: Falmer, 2000.

Brew, Angela. *The Nature of Research: Inquiry in Academic Contexts*. London: Routledge Falmer, 2001.

Bryman, Alan. *Social Science Research Methods*. Second Edition. Oxford: Oxford University Press, 2004.

Chambliss, Daniel F. & Russel K. Schutt. *Making Sense of the Social World: Methods of Investigation*. Second Edition. Thousand Oaks, California: Pine Forge Press, 2006.

Ciulla, Joanne B. "Leadership ethics: Mapping the Territory." *Business Ethics Quarterly* 5 (1995): 5–28.

Creswell, John W. *Qualitative Inquiry and Research Design: Choosing among Five Approaches*. Second Edition. Thousand Oaks, California: SAGE, 2007.

Creswell, John W. *Research Design: Qualitative, Quantitative and Mixed Methods Approaches*, Third Edition. London: SAGE, 2008.

Ferster, Judith, *Arguing through Literature: A Thematic Anthology and Guide to Academic Writing*. New York: McGraw-Hill, 2005.

Flick, Uwe. *An Introduction to qualitative Research*. London: SAGE, 2002.

Fraenkel, Jack R., Wallen, Norman E. & Hyun, Helen H. *How to Design and Evaluate Research in Education*. New York: McGraw Hill, 2012.

Gall, Meredith D., Walter R. Borg, Walter R. & Gall, Joyce P. *Educational Research: An Introduction*. Sixth Edition. White Plains, New York: Longman, 1996.

Georges, Robert A. & Jones, Michael O. *People studying People: The Human Element in Fieldwork*. Berkely: University of California Press, 1980.

Gibbins, John R. & Reimer, Bo. *The impact of Values*, edited by Jan W. van Deth and Elinor Scarbrough, 301–31. New York, Oxford University Press, 1995.

Glaser, Barney G. & Strauss, Anselm L. *The Discovery of Grounded Theory: Strategies for Qualitative Research*. New Brunswick and London: Aldine Transaction, 1967.

Gobo, Giampietro. *Doing Ethnography*. Los Angels: SAGE, 2008.

Hammersley, Martyn and Paul Atkinson. *Ethnography: Principles and Practice*, Second Edition. New York, New York: Routledge, 1995.

Hart, Chris. *Doing literature Review: Releasing the Social Science Research Imagination*. London: SAGE, 1998.

Hesse-Biber, Sharlene Nagy & Leavy, Patricia. *The Practice of Qualitative Research,* Second Edition. Los Angeles: SAGE, 2011.

Kantowitz, Barry H., Roedger III, Henry L. & Elmes, David G. *Experimental Psychology: Understanding Psychological Research*. St. Paul, New York & San Francisco: West Publishing Company, 1988.

Kee, Howard Clark. *Christian Origins in Sociological Perspective: Methods and Resources*. Philadelphia: The Westminster Press, 1980.

Kibuuka, Paul K. & Karuggah, Robert, *Certificate geography*. Oxford, New York: Oxford University Press, 2003.

Kothari, C.R. *Research Methodology: Methods and Techniques*. New Delhi: New Age International, 2004.

Kumar, Ranjit. *Research Methodology: A Step-by-step Guide for Beginners*. Second Edition. London: SAGE, 2005.

Kvale, Steinar & Brinkmann, Svend. *Interviews: Learning the Craft of Qualitative Research Interviewing*. Second Edition. London: SAGE, 2009.

Leedy, Paul D. *Practical Research: Planning and Design*. Second Edition. New York: Macmillan, 1980.

Locke, Laurence F., Silverman, Stephen J. & Spirduso, Waneen Wyrick. *Reading and Understanding Research*. Second Edition. Thousand Oaks: SAGE, 2004.

Machi, Laurence A. & McEvoy, Brenda T. *The Literature Review: Six Steps to Success*. Thousand Oaks, California: SAGE, 2009.

Mannion, Gerard. *Ecclesiology and Postmordenity: Questions for the Church in Our Time*. Collegeville, Minnesota: Liturgical Press, 2007.

Maxwell, Joseph A. *Qualitative Research Design: An Interactive Approach*. Thousand Oaks, California: SAGE, 2005.

Merriam, Sharan B. *Qualitative Research and Case Study Applications in Education: Revised and Expanded from Case Study Research in Education*. San Francisco: Jossey-Bass, 1998.

Mligo, Elia Shabani, *Jesus and the Stigmatized: Reading the Gospel of John in a Context of HIV/AIDS-Related Stigmatization in Tanzania*. Eugene, Oregon: Pickwick Publications, 2011.

Miles, Matthew B. & Hubermann, Michael A. *Qualitative data Analysis: A Sourcebook of New Methods*. Beverley Hills, California: SAGE, 1984.

Miles, Matthew B. & Hubermann, Michael A. *Qualitative Data Analysis: A Sourcebook of New Methods*. Second Edition. Thousand Oaks: SAGE, 1994.

Mouton, Johann, *How to Succeed in Your Master's and Doctoral Studies: A South African Guide and Resource Book*. Pretoria: Van Schaik, 2001.

Ndunguru, Philibert C. *Lectures on Research Methodology for Social Sciences.* Mzumbe, Morogoro: Research Information and Publication Department, 2007.

Newman, Isadore & Benz, Carolyn R. *Qualitative-quantitative Research Methodology: Exploring the Interactive Continuum.* Carbondale & Edwardsville: The Board of Trustees, Illinois University Press, 1998.

Northey, Margot, Knight, David B. & Drapper, Dianne. *Making Sense: A Student's Guide to Research and Writing.* Don Mills: Oxford University Press, 2009.

Pazmiño, Robert W. *Doing Theological Research: An Introductory Guide for Survival in Theological Education.* Eugene, Oregon: Wipf and Stock, 2009.

Rubin, Herbert J. and Rubin, Irine S. *Qualitative interviewing: The Art of hearing Data.* London: SAGE, 1995.

Seidman, Irving. *Interviewing as Qualitative Research: A Guide for Researchers in Education and Social Sciences.* New York, New York: Teachers College Press, 2006.

Swales, John M. and Feak, Christine B. *Academic Writing for Graduate Students: Essential Skills.* Second Edition. Ann Arbor, Michigan: The University of Michigan Press, 2004.

Vyhmeister, Nancy Jean. *Quality Research Papers: For Students of Religion and Theology,* Second Edition. Grand Rapids: Zondervan, 2008.

Walcott, Harry F. *The Art of Fieldwork.* Walnut Greek, California: Altamira Press, 1995.

Wilson, Jonathan. *Essentials of Business Research: A Guide to doing Your Research Project.* Los Angeles: SAGE, 2010

Yin, Robert K. *Case Study Research: Design and Methods.* Fourth Edition. London: SAGE, 2009.

www.ingramcontent.com/pod-product-compliance
Lightning Source LLC
Chambersburg PA
CBHW061739270326
41928CB00011B/2303